CEMETERY MARKER READINGS
OF
ST. PETER'S CATHOLIC CHURCH

(also known as Nanny Goat Hill Cemetery)

111 Duke St. (now known as 7th Street)
Reading, Berks County, Pennsylvania

compiled by
Edgar H. Zimmerman

Published by
Closson Press

Published by
Closson Press
1935 Sampson Drive, Apollo, PA 15613-9208
Phone: (724)-337-4482/Fax: (724)-337-9484
http://www.clossonpress.com
First Edition
ISBN #1-55856-300-8
Library of Congress Card Number 99-75167
© copyright, March 2000
Edgar H. Zimmerman/Closson Press

ST. PETER'S CEMETERY
READING, PA.

St. Peter's Cemetery was founded shortly after the church was founded by Jesuits from St. Paul's Mission, Bally, Pa. in 1752, at 111 Duke Street (now known as 7th Street.) The Cemetery continued beside the Church until 1844, when it was moved to Tenth and South Streets Reading. Other wise known as Nanny Goat Hill. The land that the Church and the Cemetery had been located on was sold in 1845 so that a new Church could be constructed on South Fifth Street.

HANNAHOE - SCHAEFFER
Ritual at St. Peter's Cemetery

Two friends that seemed to be an unlikely match were the Irishman, Thomas C. Hannahoe, born in County Mayo, Ireland in 1835 who was known as the "Mayor of Irishtown" in Reading, Pennsylvania. Who owned a bar with the patriotic name of the Stars and Stripes Saloon. Alvah Oscar Schaeffer was born in Cressona, Schuylkill County, on Mary 16, 1866, just seven and one-half hours before the advent of St. Patrick's Day. The fact that there was a 31 year difference in their age might precluded them from becoming friends.

Hannahoe apparently taken an instant liking to the German--American and put out the word that no harm was to befall his friend Alvah Schaeffer. Since there were frequent fights without siders. Hannahoe said that he was to go any where in Irishtwon that he wished to without any harm befalling him.

Most likely it was music that was at the base of their friendship. Tom was a ready singer and had a good voice. Alvah Schaeffer a proffessional muciccian, fit in very well. St. Patrick's Day was celebrated at the Stars and Striks Saloon which was always decked out all in green. With Tom Hannahoe presiding. He would usuallly dress entirely in green on St. Paddy's Day. From the top of his head to the shoes on his feet. He would be dressed in green.

On St. Patrick Day eve he would have six bartenders on hand to serve the many customers that came to see and hear the famous Tom Hannahoe sing and play his fife.

One evening Alvah strolled in the Stars and Strips Saloon with his cornet. It was either 1893 or 1894. He obliged those present with some tunes. Then, at Tom's request, he played "Lass of Galway," bringing tears to the eyes of Tom Hannahoe. At that time Hannahoe proposed a pact to his younger friend.

"If death were to take Tom first then Alvah would play the tunes "Lass of Galway" and "Nearer My God to Thee" over his grave site on St. Patrick's Day at midnight. If Alvah his friend were to predecease Tom, he would keep Alvah's grave site forever green. Another earlier version was that Tom's part of the bargain was to sing the same two songs each St. Patrick's Day at midnight over the grave site of Alvah Schaeffer.

This pact was not long in being tested as on February 10, 1897, Tom Hannahoe expired from typhoid pneumonia, aged 61 years.

Tom was buried in St. Peter's Cemetery at 11th and South Streets. Itmust have seem that the entire Irish town and friends of long standing were at his grave site for the burial. As were his friend Alvah Schaeffer and the Ringgold Band which Alvah was a member of. Men from the Washington Hook and Ladder Fire Company also were present.

On March 17, 1897, Alvah Schaeffer fulfilled his part of the pact. To anyone present it would seem that the entire populace of Irishtown were present with all of his friends. Alvah Schaeffer played the tunes that Tom Hannahoe had requested on his cornet at midnight. Little notice was taken at the time of this completing of the pact made three or so years ago.

The health of Alvah Schaeffer started to deteriorate as years passed and by 1923 he was unable to play his cornet at all. For a few years a music student played for him on St. Patrick's Day. This did not last many years and it seemed as if the pact had reached it's end. Then a reporter from the Reading Eagle convinced the ailing Schaeffer to continue the ritual with a surrogate cornetist. Alvah Schaeffer agreed and Elmer Addis a member of the Ringgold Band played for him, with Schaeffer by his side. This continued until the death of Schaeffer on March 10, 1947. He was buried at the Laureldale Cemetery, on St. Patrick's Day.

For thirty years no one taken the place of Schaeffer at the grave site of Hannahoe until the Bicentennial acttivity spearheaded by the enthusiasm of the late historian Charles Schyler Castner, and the Reading

Musical Foundation with former Police Chief Dobinski a history buff. The Hannahoe - Schaeffer pact has reached the century mark. Will it continue until the next centuary mark? I wonder.

March 18, 1998.
Edgar H. Zimmerman

NAME	BORN	DIED
- A -		
Abitabile, Domenico	1884	1918
Accordino, Antonia	5/25/1887	5/30/1913
Accordino, Carmello	3/22/1887	2/15/1943
wo Sebastian Accordino		
Accordin/o, Sammy	4/5/1918	10/1/1918
Accordino, Sebastian	8/27/1881	11/8/1951
h/o Carmello Accordino		
Adams, Joseph	12/18/1837	5/13.1882
Adams, Joseph P.	10/26/1867	1/13/1886
Albert, Anna Eva aged 29-6-10	10/20/183?	8/30/186?
Albert, Mariam	4/14/1882	1/7/1910
Albert, Matteo G.	1/14/1883	4/30/1939
Albert, William V.	1880	1959
Coxwain, U.S. Navy, Spanish American War.		
Albert, Stefana Cosentino	7/21/1887	7/7/1915
Albrecht, Charles S.	3/13/1880	4/26/1891
Albrecht, Joseph A. aged 63 years	1830	3/1/1893
Albrecht, Margaret aged 81 years	1838	3/7/1919
Albright, Annie M.	4/4/1858	1/16/1877
Albright, Elizabeth	12/16/1832	12/28/1887
Albright, Samuel	7/3/1834	1/26/1898
Albright, William F.	3/28/1858	11/9/1861
Allgaier, Catharine	5/10/185?	8/12/185?
d/o Joseph & Anna Margaret Allgaier		
Allgaier, Catharine	10/10/1737	2/10/1811
w/o Sebastian Allgaier		
Allgaier, Charles P.	5/4/1817	1/5/1911
Allgiaer, Emma Catharine	6/11/1849	12/27/1867
d/o Joseph & Anna Margaret Allgaier		
Allgaier, Francis S.	10/3/1831	8/27/1883
Allgaier, George P.	8/26/1860	9/5/1885
Allgaier, John	1853	6/30/1853
s/o Ludovico Allgaier & Sarah Diehl.		
Allgaier, John	6/26/1784	3/15/1863
Allgaier, Mary A.	11/17/1836	5 /6/1898
Allgaier, Mary D.	2/28/1814	6/23/1895
Allgaier, Mary L.	4/13/1786	11/3/1874
Allgaier, Sarah P.	4/9/1810	8/31/1890

Name	Birth	Death
Allgaier, Sebastian	3/22/1737	2/27/1816
h/o Catharine Allgaier.		
Allgaier, William S.	3/10/1808	2/4/1898
Allgaler, Anna	NBDR	NDDR
Allgaler, Augustus	NBDR	NDDR
Allgaler, Jacob	NBDR	NDDR
Allgaler, Louisa	NBDR	NDDR
Amicone, Argentina	1906	1961
Amicone, Fiorindo	1883	1972
Amicone, Rose	1906	1961
Amoroso, Frances	1876	1959
Amoroso, Gaetano D.	1871	1928
Amoroso, Matteo	1908	1908
Amoroso, Matteo	1909	1914
Amoroso, Matthies	6/2/1903	6/23/1908
Amoroso, Maria	1906	1908
Anderko, John	7/24/1912	9/1/1921
Andrejansky, John S.	1879	1976
h/o Susanna S. Andrejansky		
Andrejansky, Paul	1919	1944
Was in Armed Forces W.W. II. s/o John S. & Susanna Andrejansky.		
Andrejansky, Suanna S.	1883	1966
w/o John S. Andrejansky.		
Archer, Caroline	10/8/1875	8/24/1956
Archer, Catherine (nee McManus)	2/23/1845	11/3/1909
Archer, John M.	6/19/1872	3/6/1919
Archer, Mary	2/13/1881	3/28/1963
Arentz, Emma	1859	1910
Arentz, Francis D.	1886	1941
h/o Hannah Arentz		
Arentz, George P.	1847	1917
Arentz, Hannah (nee Gallagher)	1884	1916
w/o Francis D. Arentz.		
Arentz, John C.	NBDR	1961
Arentz, Matilda C.	1884	1967
Armao, Jennie	5/30/1925	3/25/1926
Armao, Michele	2/5/1911	9/30/1928
Arnold, Aaron P.	1848	1909
Arnold, Annie E.	1851	1902
Arnold, Eugene	1858	1893
Atsilsi, Amzina	NBDR	1917
d/o Mires & Diena Rugpuicio.		

Auchter, Anthony	7/21/1850	6/9/1890
h/o Mary Bauer who was d/o of Peter Bauer.		
Auchter, Theresa	8/8/1821	8/10/1887
Auer, Karl	1/11/1847	3/8/1913
Born Gailingen, Baden, Germany		
Auer, Maria Josephine (nee Gantert)	2/14/1850	5/19/1933
Born, Kehl, Baden, Germany.		

- B -

Baca, George	7/25/1863	1/25/1910
Bachman, Anna Fern	1/4/1919	2/23/1920
d/o Joseph & Mary Bachman.		
Bachman, Annie	4/9/1847	7/1/1910
Bachman, Carl	1887	1939
Bachman, Francis	10/25/1840	1/13/1921
h/o Margaret Bachman.		
Bachman, Francis J.	7/18.1869	8/31/1898
Bachman, George	3/10/1873	2/7/1894
Bachman, John	6/24/1836	6/18/1894
Bachman, Joseph	5/13/1901	7/24/1901
s/o Joseph & Mary Bachman.		
Bachman, Maggie	11/9/1869	5/3/1888
Bachman, Margaret	4/17/1841	4/13/1908
w/o Francis Bachman.		
Bachman, Mary	11/20/1874	11/2/1894
w/o Joseph Bachman.		
Bachman, Mary Shirley	NBDR	5/17/1929
d/o George R. & Maude M. Bachman.		
Bachman, Thomas	6/28/1916	12/23/1917
s/o Thomas & Ahenda Bachman		
Bacsa, Janos	1859	1/2/1902
Balbach - Greth, Caroline	1859	1889
Balbach - Greth, John	1866	1933
Balbach - Greth, Joseph	1855	1901
Balbach, Emma	10/31/1863	1/12/1883
Balbach, Theresa	10/14/1860	7/?/1870
Baranowski, ?	3/28/1872	2/8/1907
Bard, Elizabeth	1859	1902
Bard, Henry	1859	1898
Barrasso, Anthony J.	1910	1949
Barrasso, Antonio	1861	1935
Barrasso, Carmella	1881	1938
Barrasso, John	1885	1948
Barrasso, Madalena	1885	1963

Name	Birth	Death
Barrasso, Marie M.	12/20/1915	8/27/1963
Barrasso, Mary	1895	NDDR
Barrasso, Michael A.	1892	1980
Barrasso, Richard	1886	1931
Bartnick, Cecylia	1908	1911
Bartnick, Maryanna	1904	1908
Barto, P.E.	3/15/1912	7/16/1912
Bauer, Charles E.	6/6/1859	NDDR
Bauer, Clara M.	1875	1955
Bauer, Elizabeth	1817	1883
Bauer, Emma Elizabeth	1851	8/16/1852
Illegitimate daughter of Sarah Bauer.		
Bauer, Henry	1819	1871
Bauer, John	9/13/1824	2/21/1903
Bauer, John S.	6/28/1851	2/13/1894
Bauer, Joseph	1861	1935
h/o Katherine Bauer.		
Bauer, Katherine	1862	19---
w/o Joseph Bauer.		
Bauer, Peter	5/7/1829	NDDR
Bauer, Samuel	1867	1909
Bauer, Susanna	6/15/1808	8/4/1894
Bauer, Xavier	12/4/1806	11/25/1896
Baumcraiz, Lorenz	8/7/1818	1/22/1895
Bauneister, Martha	7/25/1821	7/21/1911
d/o Jacob & Johanna Fleckenstein. Born Bavaria, Germany.		
Baumkratz, John	12/8/1858	3/29/1892
Bechtel, John A.	May 1843	April 1891
Bechtel, Stanley W.	1904	1971
h/o Loretta K. Bechtel.		
Beck, Maria Ann (nee Juncy)	NBDR	NDDR
w/o Theobold Beck.		
Beck, Theobold	12/31/1787	6/14/1863
h/o Maria Ann Beck.		
Becker, Charles A.	7/25/1870	8/11/1919
Becker, Christopher	7/2/1844	6/2/1897
Becker, George A.	1875	1926
Becker, John andreas	11/3/1825	9/16/1874
Becker, John H.	12/25/1840	2/2/1898
Co D. 3rd Regt. Pvt. U.S. Army.		
Becker, Joseph A.	3/19/1878	10/18/1954
Becker, Lioba	6/13/1846	9/26/1915
Becker, Rosa	2/11/1841	12/17/1917
Becker, Theresa M.	9/24/1881	3/12/1955

Beil, Helen	1844	1911
Beil, Joseph	1830	1922
Beil, Maria	8/7/1876	10/2/1876
Belaire, Rene	1904	1941
Belz, Mary T. (nee Kohler)	4/6/1882	7/20/1906
Bender, Christine	11/16/1848	2/23/1882
w/o Levi Bender. Mother of George S. Bender.		
Bender, George S.	5/15/1868	3/16/1888
s/o Levi & Christine Bender.		
Bender, Levi	3/7/1845	3/2/1882
h/o Christine Bender. Father of George S. Bender.		
Bennett, Elizabeth	1869	1953
Bennett, Mary	1896	9/7/1913
Bergold, Anton	NBDR	5/20/1838
Berlinger, Carl J.	1827	1920
Berlinger, John	1866	1897
Berlinger, Margaret	1863	NDDR
Berlinger, Margaret A.	1837	1908
Bettig, Eugene	7/5/1842	10/19/1920
Bettig, Eugene L.	10/19/1869	8/17/1948
Bettig, Marie C.	8/8/1869	1/24/1923
Bettig, Theresa	11/3/1843	8/1/1894
Betinger, Lydia	1877	1898
Raised at St. Catharine's Orphange.		
Bevitch, Andrew	1888	1942
Bevitch, Anthony B.	6/19/1857	7/9/.1921
Bevitch, Eva E.	4/30/1865	10/31/1928
Biffel, Elizabeth S.	1892	1947
Billi, John	1883	10/2/1909
Billi, Zuzana	NBDR	3/28/1909
Bilski, Maryann	1860	5/7/1902
Bingaman, John	4/19/1874	8/26/1894
s/o Robert & Theresa Bingaman.		
Birmelin, Agnes S.	2/27/1859	3/24/1926
w/o George F. Birmelin.		
Birmelin, George F.	1/17/1849	8/22/1928
h/o Agnes S. Birmelin.		
Birmelin, Jennie M.	10/12/1882	3/2/1927
d/o George F. & Agnes S. Birmelin.		

Name	Born	Died
Birney, Dennis	8/12/1824	2/6/1900
Born County Antrim, Ireland. h/o Mary Jane Birney.		
Birney, Mary Jane	8/2/1826	1/6/1895
Born County Antrim,. Ireland. w/oDennis Birney.		
Birney, Peter	12/25/1864	1/27/1918
Bislema, Anna	1883	2/11/1910
Bisser, Kate (nee Kuhns)	5/11/1862	3/17/1886
w/o Henry J.W. Bisser.		
Blank, Anne	1/20/1890	7/11/1894
Blankenmiller, Maggie	5/21/1862	NDDR
Blessing, Children (2)	NBDR	NDDR
Children of John & Catharine Blessing.		
Blessing, Albert J.	7/16/1871	8/13/1872
w/o John & Catharine Blessing.		
Blessing, Balthaser	1845	1917
Blessing, Edward T.	7/2/1801	8/2/1891
Blessing, Fancis X.	8/16/1829	5/5/1900
h/o Rosa Blessing.		
Blessing, John	6/3/1829	11/30/1914
Blessing, John	7/9/1863	10/27/1885
s/o John & Catharine Blessing.		
Blessing, Joseph J.	1883	1943
s/o Balthaser & Theresa Blessing. Pvt. Bn D 67 CAC W.W. I.		
Blessing, Katharina	12/12/1828	12/3/1901
Blessing, Louisa	11/3/1859	5/31/1884
d/o John & Catharine Blessing.		
Blessing, Rosa	8/19/1823	10/7/1871
w/o Francis X Blessing.		
Blessing, Rosa	4/19/1885	9/19/1885
Blessing, Theresa	1884	1918
w/o Balthaser Blessing.		
Blessing, Veronica	8/27/1890	4/14/1907
Blessing, Wilhelmina C. (nee Klemmer)	1884	1975
Bloch, Frank	1889	1962
Bloch, Leo	NBDR	7/18/1913
Bloch, Mary T.	NBDR	1/9/1916
Bloch, Sadie R.	1893	1969
Bloch, Stephen	1881	1923
Boasstet?, Daniel	1853	7/14/1854
s/o Jacob Boasstet? & Catharina Felix.		
Bobst, Daniel	5/7/1853	?/14/187?
Bobst, Mary	8/5/1880	4/17/1881
Bodner, Joseph	NBDR	7/22/1909
Bodner, Joseph P.	NBDR	1/1/1908

Boehnlein, Sebastian	1838	3/9/1903

Member of 29th Regt. N.Y. Volunteer Infantry Civil War. h/o Victoria G. Boehnlein.

Boehnlein, Victoria G.	10/1/1837	2/22/1891

w/o Sebastian Boehnlein. Born, Ghent, Belgium.

Boehringer, George	4/23/1808	2/22/1883

h/o Sarah Boehringer.

Boeringer, Dominick	1854	6/23/1854

s/o George Boeringer & Maria Siegfried.

Boginski, Anna W. (Infant)	NBDR	1891
Boginski, Annie	10/9/1867	7/18./1903
Boginski,. Leon T.	NBDR	1892
Boginski, Ludwika	1898	1901

Boguslowski, Frank	1/23/1923	5/10/1936
Boguslowski, Joanna	7/26/1898	10/28/1948

Bohanak, John	5/8/1922	5/9/1922

Boheneck, Elizabeth	1859	1908

Bolich, Anna M.	1/1/1819	7/1/1875

w/o Michael Bolich.

Bolich, Michael	5/16/1810	9/4/1880

h/o Anna M. Bolich.

Bolognese, Frank	8/10/1912	10/10/1912
Bolognese,. John	8/10/1812	8/23/1912

Bolton, John Carol	1853	7/22/1854

s/o Benjamin Bolton & Elisabeth Eckenroth.

Books, Catharine	12/21/1868	NDDR

w/o Charles Books.

Books, Charles	8/29/1872	8/24/1913

h/o Catharine Books.

Boone, Bridget A.	1843	1/2/1895
Boone, Geroge W.	NBDR	NDDR
Boone, Thomas	1838	2/13/1894

Booz, Carolina (nee Yerger)	12/25/1860	4/10/1895

Borcky, Ann Sarah	2/24/1896	10/24/1897

d/o Joseph K. & Emma H. Borcky.

Borcky, Emma H.	1855	1917

w/o Joseph K. Borcky.

Borcky, Joseph	4/11/1818	2/15/1910

f/o Joseph K. Borcky.

Borcky, Joseph K.	1850	1913

h/o Emma H. Borcky.

Name	Birth	Death
Borcky, Lydia	3/23/1821	8/17/1905
Bordy, Adolph	1798	1886
h/o Barbara Bordy.		
Bordy, Barbara	1805	1883
w/o Adolph Bordy.		
Born, Ellen M.	1886	1889
d/o Peter E. & Anna M. Born.		
Born, John A.	7/11/1831	10/17/1907
h/o Mary A. Born. f/o Peter E. Born.		
Born, Mary A.	4/10/1834	12/19/1917
w/o John A. Born. m/o Peter E. Born.		
Borst, Elizabeth	10/14/18??	7/20/1???
d/o Jacob & Catharine Borst.		
Borst, John W.	1855	1927
Borst, Mary E.	1887	1918
Borst, Mary P.	1854	1887
Borst, William	6/7/1851	8/15/1852
Borzilleri, Rosaria	3/3/1865	7/16/1918
Bosold, Adam	1822	1894
h/o Maria Bosold.		
Bosold, Maria	2/2/1815	5/11/1866
w/o Adam Bosold.		
Boster, Joseph	9/16/1847	3/26/1864
Boster, Joseph	6/14/1811	2/4/1885
Boster, Theresa	12/18/1864	1/12/1891
Bower, Conrad G.	3/22/1846	1/22/1904
Bower, Katie	6/16/1863	6/9/1889
Bower, Sarah A.	3/6/1848	8/23/1907
Bower, Sarah Emma	2/15/1852	2/4/1856
d/o John & Lydia Bower.		
Bowers, Augustus	1887	1922
Bowers, Charles E.	4/20/1889	4/10/1934
Pvt 4th DB W.W. I.		
Bowers, John	1878	1934
Pvt Co A 4th Regt. Spanish American War.		
Boyer, Catherine H.	1/8/1867	9/17/1914
Boyer, Gertrude (nee Brady)	1889	1970
Boyer, Loretta G.	8/29/1897	6/26/1898
Boyer, Martin	4/24/1864	8/25/1909
d/o J. & E. Boyer.		
Boyer, Paul N.	1911	1968
Cpl U.S. Marine Corps W.W. II.		

Boylan, Margaret	1836	12/3/1874
Born, Cavan County, Ireland. w/o Owen Boylan.		
Boylan, Mary	1810	1881
Boylan, Sister Mary Monica	NBDR	9/7/1867
Boylan, Owen	1832	12/11/1864
Born, Cavan County, Ireland. h/o Margaret Boylan,.		
Boylan, Owen A.	1863	1904
Boyle, Sister Mary Cephas	NBDR	1/3/1867
Boyle, William F.	1827	4/7/1881
Born, Tipperary County, Ireland.		
Bradbury, Angela Virginia	8/10/1905	11/24/1929
Buried with her, is her un-named baby.		
Brady, Anna M.	1865	1945
Brady, Lucy C.	1897	1967
Brady, Magdalene	2/2/1821	4/8/1889
w/o Matthis Brady.		
Brady, Mary A.	3/15/1844	3/6/1915
w/o Thomas L. Brady.		
Brady, Matthis	8/12/1825	11/20/1898
h/o Magdalene Brady.		
Brady, Thomas L.	6/15/1841	4/8/1908
h/o Mary A. Brady.		
Brandt, William F.	9/11/1841	2/3/1885
Brawn, Anton	NBDR	7/10/1860
Brawn, Anton	3/3/1813	7/25/1863
Braun, Barbara	NBDR	2/25/1852
Braun, Frederick W.	4/17/1815	9/25/1891
Braun, Fredrick W.	1/16/1896	10/13/1899
Braun, Hendrina	6/13/1813	1/31/1885
Braun, Mary	9/27/1857	9/4/1887
Breas, Margaret (nee Liederer)	7/11/1871	4/5/1900
w/o Daniel Breas		
Breen, Andrew	NBDR	11/23/1880
Breen, Andrew D.	9/28/1866	5/16/1886
s/o David J. & Mary E. Breen		
Breen, David	1886	1904
Breen, Harry	11/29/1874	5/25/1886
s/o David J. & Mary E. Breen		
Breen, Mary E.	1842	1920
w/o David J. Breen		
Bressler, August	2/27/1822	8/11/1869
Born Elsenfeld, Bavaria, Germany		

Brestel, Catharine	1822	1906
w/o Jacob Brestel		
Brestel, Jacob	1822	1881
h/o Catharine Brestel		
Brestel, Jacob	1905	1953
Brice, Bridget	4/20/1854	10/7/1932
Brice, Charles	5/13/1849	4/11/1923
Brice, Loiuise S.	1876	1953
Brice, Mary S.	1895	1919
Brice, Michael J.	1909	1917
Brice, Michael P.	1873	1952
Brickel,. Francis	10/5/1809	5/1/1890
h/o Mary Brickel		
Brickel, Infant	NBDR	NDDR
Child of Francis & Mary Brickel		
Brickel Mary,	3/19/1825	1/5/1890
w/o Francis Brickel		
Broderick, Ellen	NBDR	NDDR
Broderick, John	1858	5/11/1893
Broderick, William	1798	10/12/1868
h/o Margaret Broderick		
Brogley, Annie E.	1879	1898
Brogley, Elias	1839	1885
Brogley, Elizabeth	1842	2/4/1912
Brogley, Emma C.	4/2/1871	1/5/1942
Brogley, Francis A.	7/8/1872	7/27/1946
Brogley, Joseph	8/17/1874	4/21/1903
Brogley, Laura V.	5/2/1874	9/25/1899
Brogley, Sarah	1843	1923
Brogley, William	1840	11/30/1905
Was in Co. G 157th Regt Pennsylvania Volunteers Civil War.		
Burke, Edward	1815	1880
h/o Mary Burke.		
Burke, Mary	1829	1895
w/o Edward Burke.		
Burkman, Coral Adam	1926	1932
Burkman, Earl F.	1925	1926
Burkman, Leona A.	1923	1925
Burkman, Paul M.	1918	1925
Burns, Clara (Orphan)	6/30/1887	9/30/1908
Burns, James	1839	5/25/1914
Burns, John J.	1914	1918
Burns, Maria	1842	2/21/1935
Burns, Sara	NBDR	8/1/1935
Burns, Thomas	6/14/1889	1/11/1890
s/o Thomas & Fredericka Burns.		

Burns, Thomas F.	NBDR	8/31/1916
Buss, Anne M	4/28/1850	8/9/1918
Buss, Frank X.	11/18/1848	8/5/1888
Butt, Katherine	1912	1933
Buttery, James H.	12/20/1884	7/15/1894
s/o James D. & Mary E. Buttery.		
Byrne, Patrick J.	1844	8/6/1913

- C -

Cadan, Sarah	NBDR	7/1/1914
w/o Thomas Cadan.		
Cadan, Thomas	12/25/1888	10/20/1904
h/o Sarah Cadan.		
Caggio, Domenico	3/14/1837	10/22/1897
Cagiano, Frank	1891	1916
Callacher, John	NBDR	NDDR
s/o Julia Callacher		
Callacher, Julia	2/23/1828	4/26/1894
Callacher, Michael	NBDR	NDDR
s/o Julia Callacher.		
Callacher, Willie	NBDR	NDDR
s/o Julia Callacher.		
Callagher, Bridget	10/20/1827	9/4/1900
w/o Daniel Callagher.		
Callagher, John	8/30/1857	12/27/1912
Callahan, Bridget M.	1876	1958
w/o Joseph L. Callahan.		
Callahan, Daniel	1871	1909
Callahan, Eleanor	1875	1902
Callahan, Joseph L.	1890	1876
Campbell, Alice	5/15/1831	7/12/1891
Campbell, William J.	10/8/1847	11/19/1867
Campion, Margaret	1826	1926
Cannon, Mary	1804	4/2/1889
Cannon, Mary	NBDR	11/25/1904
Capallo, Frank	1856	1878
Capallo, John	5/6/1822	10/2/1862
Born, Bavaria, Germany. h/o Mary A. (nee Sauer) Capallo.		

Name	Birth	Death
Capallo, Mary A.	12/1/1822	4/19/1890
Born, Bavaria, German. w/o John Capallo.		
Capallo, Mary C.	1852	1880
Capallo, William	5/3/1842	7/30/1865
Capalono, Dima	6/12/1863	4/3/1916
Cappadona, Antonino	1889	1929
Cardinale, Antonia	1856	1920
Cardinale,. Carmeno	1879	1917
Carl, Rose (nee Hassler)	11/7/1855	12/1/1890
Carlo, Michael G.	11/11/1866	4/2/1907
Case, Amanda R.	1856	1936
Case, Joseph G.	1837	1911
Cassel, Ann M.	1921	1975
Cassidy, Edith	1/7/1886	7/12/1886
Cassidy, Eleanor	3/24/1872	1/19/1919
Cassidy, Elizabeth	1851	2/6/1886
Cassidy, Elizabeth A.	12/21/1857	1/4/1920
Cassidy, Eugene	6/19/1890	6/11/1941
Cassidy, Eva A.	1886	1966
Cassidy, James	2/19/1856	6/7/1915
Cassidy, James J.	4/2/1878	1/27/1943
Cassidy, John A.	1846	7/23/1877
Cassidy, Lucy	11/6/1880	3/6/1882
Cassidy, Lucy	9/8/1883	12/13/1883
Cassidy, Margaret L.	NBDR	3/1/1821
Cassidy, Martha	11/3/1891	11/3/1891
Cassidy, Mary (nee Tiernan)	10/22/1872	5/22/1904
w/o Michael Cassidy.		
Cassidy, Michael	NBDR	10/7/1896
h/o Mary (nee Tiernan) Cassidy.		
Cassidy, Michael P.	3/10/1876	9/18/1927
Cassidy, Minnie	12/10/1875	2/10/1896
Cassidy, Miriam	11/3/1891	11/3/1891
Cassidy, Naomi	5/21/1890	7/3/1890
Cassidy, Ruth	12/13/1889	2/13/1890
Cassidy, William P.	7/21/1884	12/8/1913
Catalano, Antonio	1898	1930
Catalano, Maria aged 3 months.	NBDR	NDDR
Catalano, Maria	1906	1925
Catania, Jimmie	5/16/1907	5/3/1913
Cavanaugh, John	NBDR	10/18/1906

Name	Birth	Death
Chmielewska, Boleslawa	3/5/1897	3/2/1914
Chmielewska, Bronislawa	5/30/1859	11/22/1917
Chmielewska, Feliks	5/30/1859	9/7/1900
Chuhran, Albert A.	4/21/1882	6/21/1923
Chuhran, Andro	1850	2/20/1917
Chuhran, Barbara (nee Ravel)	3/16/1887	2/17/1940
Chuhran, Michael S.	1911	1964
Was in Armed Forces W.W. II		
Chuhran, William	2/18/1909	4/8/1909
Churico, Frank	1862	1919
h/o Rose Churico		
Churico, Rose	1874	1934
w/o Frank Churico.		
Cieri, Nicola Maria	9/15/1879	5/29/1915
Ciervo, Giovannina	5/7/1882	3/18/1915
w/o Pasquale Ciervo.		
Ciotti, Luigie	March 1878	6/3/1900
Clark, Charles L.	9/24/1906	1908
Clark, Matilda	1853	6/11/1854
d/o Peter Clark & Susanna Eckenroth		
Clark, Sarah	7/3/1859	10/9/1892
Clark, Thomas P.	3/3/1856	2/6/1916
Clay, Charles A.	8/1/1883	12/16/1887
Clay, Daniel	7/31/1837	2/4/1907
Clay, Hilary 68 years.	NBDR	NDDR
Clay, John J.	11/17/1830	9/2/1861
Clay, John L.	NBDR	8/1/1853
Clay, Joseph J.	4/13/1823	3/5/1892
Member of 88th Regt. Pa. Volunteers Civil War.		
Clay, Kate aged 12-10-22	NBDR	NDDR
Clay, Margaret	8/24/1807	11/18/1880
Clay, Mary	4/6/1828	2/20/1879
w/o Nicholas H. Clay.		
Clay, Nicholas H.	5/9/1824	1/18/1890
h/o Mary Clay.		
Clay, Sarah A.	1838	1923
Clay, William	2/18/1811	8/29/1880
Clemmer, Clara S.	NBDR	NDDR
Clemmer, Daniel J.	NBDR	NDDR
Clemmer, Edward D.	1892	1951
Clemmer, Emeline	2/23/1834	6/4/1913
Clemmer, Helen M.	1897	1968
Clemmer, James	3/26/1832	8/30/1925
Clemmer, Margaret M.	NBDR	NDDR

Clump, Edward	11/1/1875	7/24/1876
s/o Charles & Elizabeth Clump.		
Clump, Elizabeth	3/9/1843	10/1/1878
w/o Charles Clump		
Cocliuzzo, Angilo	8/6/1911	9/30/1914
Coco, Concetta	9/23/1884	2/4/1913
Coggins, Patrick	1837	1902
Co K 33rd Reg. Civil War.		
Collins, Emma E.	4/25/1899	NDDR
Collins, Harry	NBDR	1/5/1910
Collins, Mary	1825	9/20/1900 .
Born, Ballis Odare, County Sligo, Ireland.		
Collins, Mary E.	NBDR	NDDR
Collins, Patrick	1823	6/3/1894
Born, County Mayo, Ireland.		
Collins, Thomas	4/19./1862	12/23/1876
Conklin, Willie	8/9/1889	12/18/1893
s/o John & Catharine Conklin.		
Connelly, Michael P.	1866	1912
Conner, Alice	1864	1945
Conner, Edward J.	1862	1922
Conner, May A.	1860	1923
Conner, Sarah (nee Clay)	2/3/1828	8/21/1888
Connolly, Cecelia	1/10/1869	7/10/1869
d/o Peter & Mry Connolly.		
Connolly, James Patrick	3/7/1879	7/7/1879
Connolly, Mary	NBDR	2/5/1912
w/o Peter Connolly.		
Connolly, Peter	7/15/1842	1/31/1894
h/o Mary Connolly. Born, County Tyrone, Ireland.		
Conrad, Grave (marker broken)	4/26/1867	4/11/1887
Conrad, Anna M.	1880	1915
Conrad, Benedict	1829	1887
Conrad, Romain J. Sr.	1876	1967
Conrad, Romain J. Jr.	1913	1916
Conrad, Thekla	1824	1892
Conrad, William M.	1915	1944
KIA W.W. II. Buried in France..		
Constantino, Salvatore	1/25/1868	7/3/1932
Convry, Bernard T.	12/27/1905	7/27/1924
s/o John F. & Catherine G. Convry.		

Name	Birth	Death
Convry, Francis W.	8/15/1901	8/21/1974
s/o John f. & Catherine G. Convry.		
Convry, John F.	6/25/1871	2/2/1909
h/o Catherine G. Convry.		
Conway, Clara (nee Foster)	1884	1955
Conway, Edward	NBDR	NDDR
Conway, John	NBDR	NDDR
Conway, Patrick Eugene	1874	1944
Conway, Thomas	NBDR	NDDR
Cook, Caroline	5/12/1835	12/27/1902
Cook, John	8/9/1837	11/6/1905
Cook, Verna L.	2/28/1898	7/24/1971
Cook, William E.	10/8/1895	3/7/1976
Cooney, Catharine T.	1897	1938
Cooney, Ellen A.	1894	1952
Cooney, Edward	1850	1930
Cooney, Margaret	1861	1932
Cooney, Margaret E.	1895	1964
Cooney, Mary	1820	1869
Cooney, Patrick	1852	1920
Cooney, William	1810	1899
Born, Leix, County Queens, Ireland.		
Coppinger, Catharine	NBDR	6/2/1940
Coppinger, John P.	5/17/1876	10/31/1904
Coppinger, Margaret (nee Duffy)	NBDR	8/21/1916
w/o Michael Coppinger.		
Coppinger, Michael	1836	9/11/1896
h/o Margaret (nee Duffy) Coppinger.		
Coppinger, Michael J.	3/20/1879	7/21/1902
Corbly, Ann	NBDR	11/21/1915
Corbly, Bernard F.	NBDR	2/20/1943
Corbly, Margaret C.	NBDR	5/3/1953
Corbly, Patrick	NBDR	3/8/1909
Corbly, Thomas	NBDR	10/8/1903
Corcoran, Amelia	1874	1949
Cosgrove, Mary A.	NBDR	11/3/1871
w /o Patgrick Cosgrove.		
Cosgrove, Patrick	NBDR	Sept 1859
h /o Mary A. Cosgrove.		
Coyle, Edward J.	1882	1913
Craszmann, Katharina (nee Bechtels)	1/22/1829	3/12/1859
w/o Franz Craszmann.		

Name		
Crimaldi, Numziata Iannagi	1852	1928
w/o Gaetano Crimaldi.		
Crimaldi, Salavatore	1883	1946
Crimmens, Alice	1835	5/21/1910
Crimmens, Alice A.	NBDR	8/18/1949
Crimmens, John	1831	5/11/1906
Crimmens, Kate J.	NBDR	2/7/1867
Crimmens, Peter	NBDR	2/5/1916
Crinkshank, Daniel A.	11/5/1836	7/10/1910
Crinkshank, J. W.	1873	1909
Crinkshank, Margaret T.	10/18/1843	NDDR
Crispin, Charles W.	1848	1878
Crispin, Mary P.	1823	1909
Croll, Catherine	5/23/1822	Dec.1882
Croll, Joseph	1/31/1819	12/31/1897
Croll, Peter 7 months old.	NBDR	1863
Cronan, Agnes A.	1882	1958
Cronan, Anna E.	6/29/1851	8/10/1905
w/o Thomas Cronan.		
Cronan, Edward	NBDR	NDDR
s/o Thomas & Anna E. Cronan.		
Cronan, Raphael	1914	1940
Cronan, Raymond	NBDR	NDDR
s/o Thomas & Anna E. Cronan.		
Cronan, Thomas J.	2/26/1852	4/4/1904
h/o Anna E. Cronan.		
Cronauer, Frederick	1885	1903
Cronauer, Joseph	1844	1924
Cronauer, Sabina	1850	1921
Cronauer, William	1877	1918
Cronon, Charlie	NBDR	NDDR
s/o Thomas Cronon		
Crook, Adam	1851	1872
Crook, Carolina	1891	1944
Crook, Charles	1813	1878
Crook, Elizabeth	1813	1877
Crook, Francis A.	1854	1932
Crook, Honora (nee Reilly)	1856	1936
Crossman, Mary M. (nee Rebhots)	2/28/1843	10/24/1902
Crossman, Michael	5/25/1860	10/17/1901
Crossmann, Francis	7/9/1827	5/1/1905
Cruseck, Mary ann	5/5/1820	1/27/1907

Ctzel, Christop	8/21/1812	1/7/1890
Ctzel, Johann	12/6/1825	4/23/1904
Ctzel, Maria	12/4/1827	12/10/1894
Cullen, Anthony	1920	1920
Cullen, Bridget	11/3/1849	2/22/1878
w/o Thomas C. Cullen.		
Cullen, Elllen	1849	1923
Sister of Thomas C. Cullen.		
Cullen, John	1848	1922
Was in Co B 205th Inf Regt Pa Volunteer's.		
Cullen, Loretta C.	1869	1945.
d/o Thomas C. & Bridget Cullen.		
Cullen, Margaret M.	12/15/1894	1/27/1975
Cullen, Mary H.	1846	1905
Cullen, Paul	1892	1895
Cullen, Peter	1845	1925
Sgt. Co B 93rd Inf Regt PA Volunteer's.		
Cullen, Vincent J.	1871	1890
Curallo, Maria	1913	1918
Curcak, Kate	1865	3/29/1907
Curcak, Michael	1847	11/29/1903
Cusano, Josephine	1873	2/9/1915
Cutler, Alberta	7/18/1900	12/29/1900
Cutler, Joseph J.	1862	1924
Cutler, Michael	1867	1936
Pvt Co C 12th Inf S.A. War.		

- D -

Dadamio, William	2/27/1911	9/29/1911
Dadamio, Carmele	NBDR	1906
Dagorska, Eva	1867	1898
D'Agostino, Maria	1916	1917
Dallevig, Charles E.	1/6/1860	6/2/1892
Dalton, Mary (nee Folest)	4/9/1830	12/5/1900
Born, County Kildare, Ireland. w/o James Dalton.		
Damato, Annie	7/26/1912	6/12/1916
Damato, Caterina	1/18/1871	3/19/1925
Damato, Francesco	1867	1944
h/o Vincenza Damato.		
D'Andrea, Luigi	1861	1913
Darenbacher, Oena (nee Steigerwald)	1887	1921

Name	Birth	Death
Davial, Georgianna (Orphan)	3/23/1891	6/28/1891
DeAngelis, John	4/9/1914	1/5/1916
DeAngelis, Angelina	1880	1925
DeAngelo, Carmela	NBDR	2/9/1908
DeChamplain, Martina	9/17/1904	12/28/1911
Decker, John	1/6/1909	8/13/1983
DeHart, Elizabeth C.	1910	1965
Deihm, ?	?/22/1792	2/9/1880
DeLay, Dorothy	NBDR	NDDR
DeLay, Ellen	NBDR	NDDR
DeLay, Henrietta	NBDR	NDDR
DeLay, Henrietta	1852	1940
DeLay, James	NBDR	NDDR
DeLay, James K.	1844	1923
DeLay, Jeremiah	1880	1971
DeLay, Jerry	NBDR	NDDR
DeLay, Roger	NBDR	NDDR
DeLay, Thomas	NBDR	NDDR
Dell, Annie, M.	10/15/1865	10/30/1916
Dell, Edward C.	4/1/1895	12/2/1953

    Cpl W.W. I   Fire-Chief; 1948 to 1953, Reading, Pa.

Name	Birth	Death
Dell, Joseph J.	1891	1967
Delorenzo, Josephine	1872	1951
Dempsey, Charles J.,	1855	1914
DeMusis, Anna	1/26/1898	11/8/1909
Denbowski, Bernard	1888	1931
Denbowski, Mary R.	1891	NDDR
Deppen, Augusta F	8/10/1881	6/12/1943
Deppen, Catharine	10/5/1806	3/15/1893

        w/o Dr. Daniel Deppen.

Name	Birth	Death
Deppen, Catharine (nee Felix)	1/26/1853	7/20/1932

        w/o William P. Deppen.

Name	Birth	Death
Deppen, Elizabeth E.	1843	1915
Deppen, Emily C.	1846	1893
Deppen, Olga G.	11/1/1896	3/8/1967
Deppen, William P.	3/27/1851	8/23/1920

        h/o Catharine (nee Felix) Deppen.

Name	Birth	Death
DeSantis, Caspar Domenica	NBDR	4/11/1912

Detombel, ?	8/30/1818	12/26/1897
Detombel, George	12/21/1850	11/23/1919
Detombel, Magdalene	11/19/1827	12/20/1910
DeVille, William E.	4/6/1862	8/9/1912
Devine, Edward	2/10/1815	7/7/1887
h/o Jane Devine.		
Devine, Ellen	1863	1892
Devine, Jane	1826	5/26/1895
w/o Edward Devine.		
Devine, John	1/27/1851	7/29/1906
Brother of Joseph Devine.		
Devine, Joseph	3/28/1858	4/11/1895
Brother of John Devine.		
Devine, Margaret A.	1859	1930
Devine, Mary	2/7/1864	3/2/1895
w/o Thomas A. Devine.		
Devine, Thomas A.	1855	1941
h/o Mary Devine.		
Devlin, John	10/15/1824	11/28/1884
h/o Mary Devlin.		
Devlin, Mary	8/1/1813	8/1/1900
w/o John Devlin.		
Deysher, Susan (nee Heisler)	11/11/1841	8/26/1888
w/o William G. Deysher.		
Deysher, William G.	9/6/1838	7/20/1913
h/o Susan (nee Heisler) Deysher.		
Dianna, Philomena	1856	1946
Dibartolmeo, Meneca Mancino	1/28/1917	2/23/1917
Dibartolmeo, Pietro S.	12/6/18??	12/10/18??
DiBlasi, Carmelo R.	8/25/1917	9/6/1917
DiBlasi, Carmello	1890	1932
DiBlasi, Frances L. (nee DeVille)	1900	1918
DiBlasi, Maria	1891	1958
DiBlasi, Melina	1892	1917
DiCarlo, Raffaele	7/28/1880	6/18/1916
Born, Abruzzi, Italy.		
Dickenson, Rose Rehrer	1888	1957
DiGiuseppe, Andreo Consentino	6/25/1917	10/16/1918
DiGiuseppe, Nicola Mirenna	4/16/1921	11/6/1926
Dilillo, Mary	5/25/1911	9/27/1913

Name	Birth	Death
Dillich, Agnes L. (nee Cronan) d/o Thomas Dillich.	1874	1932
Dilorenzo, Pasquale	3/5/1894	7/10/1913
DiMaio, Carmelo s/o Vito & Eleanor DeMaio.	3/19/1920	8/28/1920
DiMascio, Rosaria	1/29/1880	7/14/1944
DiMascio, Valentino J.	8/12/1870	11/29/1942
Dinkel, George M.	1/7/1867	11/2/1893
DiPanolo, Frank	4/29/1910	3/6/1913
DiPietro, Carmelo	2/22/1887	9/17/1925
DiPietro, Dominca	7/5/1924	7/15/1925
DiRaola, Rosario	9/13/1877	7/23/1917
DiStasio, Frank	1/26/1901	6/3/1905
DiStasio, Mary	1863	1910
DiStasio, Ralph	1859	1947
DiVine, R.M.	1877	1924
DiLerbein, Maria aged 51-8-25	1837	1888
Dogorski, Antoni	1864	1925
Dogorski, Maryanna	1853	1941
Dolan, Michael	1840	8/11/1907
Dolecki, Mateusz	1833	1926
Domagalska, Mary A.	1876	1926
Danahue, Anna	1834	1906
Donahue, Clara	NBDR	NDDR
Donahue, Ellen	2/12/1863	7/1/1869
Donahue, James	1831	1883
Donahue, Patrick	4/1/1838	4/12/1900
Donatongleo, Giueppe Piluso	3/20/1877	4/9/1907
Donlon, Catharine	1846	12/28/1916
Donlon, Thomas Born, County Lonford, Ireland.	1838	3/16/1892
Dorcsak, Julia	1903	1905
Dorcsak, Mary	1872	1944
Dorcsak, Michael	1868	1928

Dosznota, Stasz	1914	8/27/1914
Dougherty, P. Alice w/o P. Dougherty.	NBDR	10/19/1911
Dougherty, Andrew J.	NBDR	4/7/1916
Dougherty, Ellen	NBDR	4/10/1921
Dougherty, James M.	NBDR	10/2/1918
Dougherty, Michael	NBDR	10/29/1919
Dougherty, Sarah T.	3/17/1840	7/2/1918
Doyle, Ann	1835	1901
Doyle, Frances H.	7/21/1849	11/11/1914
Doyle, Frank	1858	1933
Doyle, James A.	11/28/1845	12/8/1913
Doyle, James A.	1872	1895
Doyle, Joseph A.	1876	1892
Doyle, Michael Jr.	1854	1897
Doyle, Michael Sr.	1819	1894
Doyle, Patrick	1853	1933
Doyle, Thomas M. Served in Co M 12th Inf. S.A. War.	1878	1899
Dragan, Mary	1869	1955
Dragan, Mary Lesko	1893	1925
Drake, Helena d/o John & Elizabeth Drake.	2/7/1871	6/7/1876
Drake, John	7/25/1825	7/20/1879
Driscoll, Agnes M.	9/6/1857	8/30/1942
Driscoll, Anna	9/24/1858	6/7/1861
Driscoll, Catharine	10/13/1856	12/11/1919
Driscoll, Daniel J.	8/12/1824	7/14/1894
Driscoll, Daniel J.	12/24/1862	3/28/1919
Driscoll, Elizabeth	6/17/1853	9/17/1853
Driscoll, Elizabeth M.	12/20/1826	9/24/1905
Driscoll, Helen M.	9/24/1854	11/4/1898
Driscoll, James	1826	1917
Driscoll, James D.	1/5/1848	3/23/1882
Driscoll, Johanna V.	7/25/1865	10/13/1918
Driscoll, Rev. John A.	10/14/1867	11/24/1896
Driscoll, Joseph	12/5/1869	8/18/1870
Driscoll, Joseph D.	7/5/1871	6/28/1872
Driscoll, Margaret E.	9/28/1851	8/28/1871
Driscoll, Mary E.	7/28/1849	12/28/1871
Droseall, Elisabeth d/o Julis Droscall & Elisabeth Grady.	1853	9/19/1853
Drumm, Elizabeth	12/24/1778	7/27/1878
Druzba, Celia	1905	1960
Druzba, Frank	1902	1978

Name	Birth	Death
Duddy, Elizabeth	NBDR	NDDR
Duddy, Francis B.	1865	1931
Duffy, Bernard	3/8/1833	4/4/1904
Duffy, Catharine	NBDR	1/6/1889
m/o Margaret Coppinger.		
Duffy, Mary	5/18/1842	8/28/1905
Dunder, Margaret	2/4/1860	9/1/1897
w/o John Dunder.		
Dunkle, Mary A. (nee Ganter)	1877	1953
Dunn, Anna aged 32 years.	NBDR	NDDR
Dunn, Augustus aged 25 years	NBDR	NDDR
Dunn, Cecelia aged 58 years	1860	9/28/1918
w/o James J. Dunn.		
Dunn, Ellen aged 57 years	NBDR	NDDR
Dunn, Ellen aged 77 years.	NBDR	NDDR
Dunn, James J. aged 38 years.	1862	5/11/1900
Dunn, John	NBDR	NDDR
Dunn, Mary aged 21 years.	NBDR	NDDR
Dunn, Mary C.	9/22/1889	1/9/1905
Dunn, Robert aged 21 years.	NBDR	NDDR
Dunn, Thomas	NBDR	NDDR
Duser, Jacob	2/5/1828	3/6/1916
Duser, Susanna	6/15/1826	4/6/1902
Duser, William	2/28/1863	4/12/1890
Dvorscsak, Enni	7/26/1893	5/21/1916
Dwight, Charles J.	1870	1913
Dwight, Charlotte J.	1877	1961

- E -

Name	Birth	Death
Ebuer, Johann Baptist	6/3/1797	2/24/1875
Born, Eispel Groszh, Baden, Germany.		
Eck, Wilson T.	3/23/1853	NDDR
s/o George Eck & Maria M. Bernt/Berndt.		
Eckenroad, Adam	1/15/1831	7/25/1910
Eckenroad, Charistian	8/8/1833	1/28/1902
Eckenroth, Elizabeth	NBDR	1/10/1894
Eckenroth, Eva	NBDR	March 1898
Eckenroth, Henry E.	NBDR	12/8/1906
Eckenroth, John	11/11/1822	11/30/1894
h/o Mary Eckenroth.		
Eckenroth, Mary	11/22/1830	3/29/1878
w/o John Eckenroth.		

Edel, Jane M.	Dec. 1839	5/23/1874
w/o Victor Edel.		
Edinger Mary	6/8/1857	3/16/1905
Eiler, Anna W.	1866	1944
Eiler, Edward T.	1890	1960
Eiler, Johann	2/17/1819	5/31/1889
h/o Katherine Eiler.		
Eiler, Katherine	5/17/1826	8/1/1898
w/o Johann Eiler.		
Eiler, Sarah Ann	12/1/1856	4/23/1912
w/o Thomas Eiler.		
Eiler, Thomas	4/22/1855	3/23/1899
h/o Sarah Ann Eiler.		
Eisenhauer, Catharine	8/3/1817	10/26/1896
Eisenhauer, William	11/5/1811	8/30/1897
Eitzmann, John J.	12/20/1880	3/4/1882
Elbert, Christina	6/7/1866	6/16/1892
Elbert, George	7/20/1871	8/26/1890
Elbert, George A.	3/13/1829	11/12/1896
Elbert, John	8/15/1827	12/24/1912
Elbert, Magdalena	1/4/1832	6/22/1871
Elbert, Margareta	10/22/1841	7/14/1910
Elbert, Theresia	12/16/1833	8/19/1906
Elliott, Harry aged 10 months.	NBDR	NDDR
Elliot, William H.	4/8/1884	4/15/1901
Eltz, Charles J.	7/25/1861	6/3/1901
Eltz, Jacob	8/7/1808	2/14/1873
h/o Mary Eltz.		
Eltz, Katie D.	5/1/1861	3/27/1919
Eltz, Mary	1/27/1808	5/27/1873
w/o Jacob Eltz.		
Eltz, Mary	1864	9/2/1879
d/o Robert Eltz.		
Eltz, Robert	12/15/1840	12/23/1875
Eltz, Robert aged 2-5-0	NBDR	1882
Ely, Children	NBDR	NDDR
c/o John & Emma Ely.		
Ely, Conrad Edwin	9/23/1870	9/15/1877
Ely, John Pius	9/13/1871	9/29/1877
Ely, Joseph Michael	1/22/1871	9/30/1877
Ennis, James	3/15/1812	5/9/1883
Ennis, Mary	3/17/1834	3/20/1901

Enzman, Howard B.	1902	1962
Enzman, Joseph b.	1/9/1873	3/12/1916
Enzman, Lillian M.	10/20/1877	12/19/1910
Enzman, Theresa M.	5/13/1890	7/8/1979
Enzman, Dienisius	8/2/1846	12/19/1902
Enzman, John J.	10/28/1879	11/7/1912
Enzman, Joseph G.	1882	1962
Enzman, William H.	1886	1941
Corp Ordnance Dept W.W. I.		
Erlacher, Eugenia R.	NBDR	NDDR
Erlacher, George J.	1886	1959
Erlacher, George Paul	2/5/1888	2/5/1959
Pvt Bn D 3rd PA 6th Div W.W. I.		
Erlacher Jefferson	1917	1881
Born, Baden, Germany.		
Erlacher, Matilda	1841	1912
Erlacher, Raymond J.	1890	1944
Ernst, Agnes	NBDR	NDDR
Ernst, Agnes M.	2/20/1875	12/7/1880
Ernst, Edward	9/5/1880	12/5/1881
Ernst, Elizabeth	4/19/1867	8/10/1882
Ernst, Lena	3/14/1877	10/23/1893
Ernst, Margarette	6/9/1872	3/26/1886
Ernst, Mary	9/30/1864	9/18/1881
Ernst, Matilda	10/6/1868	4/15/1886
Ertel, A. Katherine	1863	1901
w/o John J. Ertel.		
Ertel, Appolonia	1844	1920
Ertel, Barbara A.	4/26/1885	9/27/1899
Ertel, George	1835	1893
Ertel, John J.	1868	1929
Ertel, Joseph	9/13/1869	4/13/1899
h/o Clara (nee Lang) Ertel.		
Eschedor, Rose	1886	1969
Etzel, George M.	1/18/1879	5/31/1888
s/o Jacob & Mary Etzel.		
Etzel, Jacob	10/21/1851	7/14/1903
h/o Mary Etzel.		
Euler, Thomas	1853	8/10/1853
s/o John Euler & Catharina Steigerwald.		
Evans, Frances Gertrude	1881	1916
w/o Frederick Evans.		
Evie?, Johan Jake	1/10/1909	11/11/1911

- F -

Falkiewicz, Leonora	3/10/1849	NDDR
Falkiewicz, Stefan	1868	NDDR
Farino, Carmela (nee Todaro)	7/22/1888	11/9/1910
Farrell, Mary (nee McManus)	1841	1/2/1914
w/o Peter Farrell.		
Farrell, Peter	1832	7/28/1899
h/o Mary (nee McManus) Farrell.		
Faust, Jasper H.	1860	11/9/1921
h/o Sallie Faust.		
Faust, Mary M.	1841	1899
w/o Charles F. Faust.		
Faust, Sallie	1863	4/14/1912
w/o Jasper H. Faust.		
Fay, Kate	NBDR	1/15/1904
Fay, Michael	NBDR	4/21/1909
Fedinecz, John	1825	12/22/1909
Feeney, Michael F.	NBDR	3/19/1925
Feldman, George	NBDR	NDDR
Feldman, George P.	1888	1950
Feldman, Mary L.	1853	1906
Felix, Ann A.	NBDR	NDDR
Felix, Anna Catharine	10/17/1827	6/24/1909
w/o Nicholas A. Felix.		
Felix, Ann Jane Lee	NBDR	NDDR
Felix, Anna M.	1/6/1859	10/30/1938
Felix, Anthony	7/29/1781	9/18/1863
h/o Catharine Felix.		
Felix, Anthony A.	2/5/1834	1/23/1889
Felix, Apolonia	1823	7/23/1887
Felix, Catharine	5/4/1788	12/4/1861
w/o Anthony Felix		
Felix, Catharine	4/10/1832	5/6/1923
Felix, Catharine Jane	1822	1/28/1869
w/o Anthony S. Felix.		
Felix, Charles	5/25/1866	2/12/1892
h/o Mary (nee Brogley) Felix.		
Felix, Gertrude M.	1889	1925
Felix, Henry	1816	10/31/1866
Felix, Jacob	3/19/1815	12/19/1909
Felix, John	1820	4/20/1884
Felix, John	1860	1896
Felix, Mary (nee Brogley.)	2/2/1867	4/9/1913
w/o Charles Felix.		

Name	NBDR	NDDR
Felix, Mary A aged 48-9-11.	NBDR	NDDR
Felix, Mary E.	7/17/1823	7/29/1883
Felix, Mary R.	NBDR	5/22/1916
Felix, Nicholas	1784	1812
Felix, Nicholas A.	2/7/1824	8/11/1874
Felix, Sarah	2/26/1830	11/15/1862
Ferguson, A. Mary (nee Deppen)	1880	1947
Ferretti, Adeline	NBDR	NDDR
Ferretti, Ernest	10/25/1940	1/23/1942
Fertsch, Edward P.	1874	1964
Fertsch, Rose T.	1880	1957
Feyrer, Johann	6/1/1843	3/11/1892
h/o Margaretha Feyrer.		
Feyrer, Margaretha	5/16/1845	3/14/1896
w/o Johann Feyrer.		
Fialkowski, A;ysius	1908	1929
Fialkowski, Bernice	1925	1935
Fialkowski, Josephine	1875	1952
Fidler, Rose	1857	1910
Figlio, Antonio	3/22/1910	4/7/1910
Filangiero, Antonio	3/4/1860	1/4/1941
Filangiero, Carmela	7/2/1857	2/20/1932
Files, Maria (nee Schmitt)	9/21/1862	10/16/1899
Finn, James H.	NBDR	5/29/1883
Finn, Charles F.	1/27/1876	5/11/1905
Finucchiaro, Teresa	11/6/1876	5/25/1917
d/o G. & R. Finucchiaro.		
Fischer, Gordian	5/12/1836	1/17/1908
h/o Kresenzia Fischer.		
Fischer, Kresenzia	2/10/1842	9/20/1899
w/o Gordian Fischer.		
Fischer, Pauline H.	4/11/1865	11/24/1893
Fisher, Catherine (nee O'Neill)	1878	1910
Fisher, Esther K.	9/9/1885	3/22/1886
Flamm, Anna E.	1874	1933
w/o William A. Flamm.		
Flamm, Edwin E.	1911	1928
s/o William A. & Anna E. Flamm.		

Name	Birth	Death
Flamm, Ferdinand	1841	1876
h/o Sarah S. Flamm.		
Flamm, Joseph A.	11/22/1875	5/22/1876
s/o Ferdinand & Sarah S. Flamm.		
Flamm, Leo M.	1895	1980
Flamm, Sarah S.	1845	1923
w/o Ferdinand Flamm.		
Flamm, Victoria	2/14/1814	12/21/1888
w/o Anton Flamm.		
Flamm, William A.	1870	1944
h/o Anna E. Flamm.		
Flanagan, Katherine E.	11/28/1864	3/25/1909
Fleckenstein, John A.	7/3/1826	4/16/1898
h/o Mary E. Fleckenstein.		
Fleckenstein, Mary E.	6/26/1826	1/30/1868
w/o John A. Fleckenstein.		
Fleming, Patrick	12/20/1839	9/11/1884
Flemming, James	NBDR	1/21/1929
Flemming, Mary	NBDR	1/27/1959
Flemming, Mary E.	NBDR	NDDR
Flemming, Michael	NBDR	NDDR
Flemming Rose	NBDR	NDDR
Flood, Anna	1825	1889
Flood, Catharine	1854	1926
Flood, Francis	1823	1878
Flood, Frank K.	1858	1916
Focht, Bertha C. (nee Huck)	1883	1915
Focht, George J.	1915	1915
Focht, Sayde (nee McDevitt)	1882	1976
Fogerty, Irene Mary	11/14/1909	2/18/1913
Foley, Anna	NBDR	3/23/1931
Foley, Bessie L.	1882	1937
Foley, Dennis	NBDR	NDDR
Foley, Lawrence	NBDR	12/11/1931
Foreman, Paul S.	1898	1955
Pvt Medical Corps 6th Inf W.W. I. h/o Rose (nee Sacco) Foreman.		
Forster, Charles J.	11/4/1830	1/10/1908
Forster, Eva T.	8/15/1853	2/28/1890
Forster, Henrietta	11/15/1842	1/1/1873
Fox, Margareta A.	1858	1911
w/o Ezekiel Fox.		

Name	Birth	Death
Franckowiak, Andrew	1895	1919
Franckowiak, John	1889	1907
Franckowiak, Katarzyna	1860	1943
Franckowiak, Stanislaw R.	1855	1919
Franco, Anthony	1915	1916
Frank, Pepe	1901	1903
Franz, Barbara	3/17/1837	2/21/1909
Born, Bayern, Germany.		
Franz, Maria T.	10/15/1861	3/17/1869
Franz, Michael	7/24/1835	5/7/1877
Born, Bayern, Germany.		
Franz, Michael A.	1877	1972
Franz, Winifred (nee McHale)	1880	1962
Frasso, Marie	4/20/1903	11/9/1909
Friday, Isabella Estella	NBDR	10/24/1880
Infant d/o Lee & Mary E. Friday.		
Friday, Martha	5/6/1895	3/3/1913
d/o Lee & Mary E. Friday.		
Fries, ?	9/1/1882	1/16/1883
Fries, Annastasia	3/26/1854	12/25/1883
w/o J.W. Fries.		
Fries, Edward C.	6/11/1875	12/21/1918
Fries, Francis W.	6/2/1877	7/28/1905
Fries, J. William	1850	1933
h/o Annastasia Fries.		
Fries, Jacob	1853	8/26/1853
s/o John Fries & M. Magdalena Berninger.		
Fries, John	7/10/1808	1/14/1883
h/o Mary M. Fries.		
Fries, Katharina	1832	11/23/1896
Fries, Mary	1851	1927
Fries, Mary M.	5/3/1808	3/8/1876
w/o John Fries.		
Fries, Walter	NBDR	6/14/1883
s/o J.W. & Annastasia Fries.		
Frischeis, Mathias	1809	1894
Inscribed on Klemmer stone.		
Fritschey, Barbara	NBDR	1900
Fritschey, Felix	1/14/1833	7/17/1902
Fritschey, John	NBDR	1899
Fuoco, Rosalia	1895	1954
Fuoco, Vito	1883	1963

Fuoti, Carmels	1890	1968
Fuoti, Gaetano	7/24/1908	5/30/1914
Fuoti, Gaetano	4/18/1915	4/18/1915
Fuoti, Joseph	1883	1932
Fuoti, Vincenza	12/23/1858	12/16/1943
Fuoti, Vincenza	8/15/1861	12/29/1969
Fuspocina, Weronika	Nov. 1909	Oct. 1915

- G -

Gable, Amelia E.	3/9/1853	11/18/1898
w/o Sebastian Gable.		
Gable, Andrew	4/28/1883	7/25/1899
s/o Sebastian & Amelia E. Gable.		
Gable, Charles A.	1879	11/18/1902
s/o Sebastian & Amelia E. Gable.		
Gable, Sebastian	9/24/1850	1/2/1911
h/o Amelia E. Gable.		
Gabor, Michael	5/3/1907	4/30/1917
Gabriel, D.	5/10/1782	3/8/1875
Gaffney, Mary	10/10/1833	7/16/1913
Gagnor, Thomas	NBDR	7/31/1853
s/o Jacob Gagnor & M. Anna McLaughlin.		
Gajewski, Boleslau	1904	1913
Gajewski, Frances	NBDR	1957
Gajewski, Vincent	NBDR	1951
Gallaghan, Dennis	1812	8/12/1851
Born, County Cork, Ireland. h/o Elizabeth (nee Brennan) Gallaghan.		
Gallaghan, Elizabeth (nee Brennan)	1811	7/1/1893
w/o Dennis Gallaghan. Born, County Cork, Ireland.		
Gallaghan, Elizabeth J.	12/13/1841	4/23/1928
Gallergher, Mary	NBDR	1/15/1872
Gallman, John	1851	3/3/1904
Gallamn, Sadie	1843	4/28/1916
Gambria, Angiola Bucci	6/16/1889	6/5/1909
Ganster, Catharine a.	1/2/1843	3/3/1902
Ganster, Christopher	2/6/1835	5/22/1901
Ganster, Ella W.	1867	1932
w/o Dr. William F. Ganster.		
Ganster, Margaret J.	2/21/1886	11/6/1909
Ganster, Teresa	9/2/1835	3/28/1873

Ganster, William F. Dr.   7/2/1865   2/11/1913
    h/o Ella W. Ganster.

Ganter, Barbara   1/23/1828   NDDR
    w/o Johann Ganter.
Ganter, Ellen L. (nee Werner)   1854   1937
Ganter, Francis   5/7/1861   9/3/1891
    s/o Francis X. & Farina Ganter.
Ganter, Francis X.   1850   1913
    h/o Farina Ganter.
Ganter, Franz Xavier   12/13/1818   3/27/1868
Ganter, Frederick W.   1879   1881
Ganter, Joseph A.   10/28/1825
    h/o Theresia Bucher.
Ganter, Mary Maria   NBDR   NDDR
Ganter, Maria   3/16/1852   4/16/1852
    d/o Joseph A. Theresia (nee Bucher) Ganter.
Ganter, Philip   NBDR   NDDR
Ganter, Theresia (nee Bucher)   10/12/1827   1/14/1898
    w/o Joseph A. Ganter.
Ganter, ?   1871   1876

Gantert, Maria A.   7/4/1815   1/6/1893

Gardner, Catharine (nee Bunty)   NBDR   2/3/1882
    w/o Jacob Gardner.
Gardner, Jacob   NBDR   NDDR
    h/o Catharine (nee Bunty) Gardner.
Gardner, Josephine Annie   NBDR   3/26/1921
    d/o Jacob & Catharine (nee Bunty) Gardner.
Gardner, Lewis Jacob   NBDR   10/30/1895
    s/o Jacob & Catharine (nee Bunty) Gardner.
Gardner, Mary Matilda   NBDR   4/19/1915
    d/o Jacob & Catharine (nee Bunty) Gardner.

Garner, Helen M.   1893   1962
Garner, Robert W.   1899   1968
    Buglar Co C 153rd Regt. W.W. I.

Garrigan, Edward J.   1/1/1834   1/14/1892
    Born, County Meath, Ireland.

Gauvreau, Mary L.   1871   1940

Gazzereo, Franceaco   10/?/1873   3/28/1911

Gebolld, Georg   4/7/1861   2/27/1882

Gegenfurtner, ?   NBDR   NDDR

Gegenheimer, Maggie   1851   1915
Gegenheimer, Rosa M.   1/17/1874   2/26/1893
    d/o John J. & Margaret Gegenheimer.

Name	Birth	Death
Gehris, Catharine	9/7/1849	4/6/1901
Gehris, Lafayette	8/14/1846	5/20/1896
Geis, Conrad	1813	1886
h/o Mary A. Geis.		
Geis, Mary A.	1825	1915
w/o Conrad Geis.		
Gerhard, Laura C. (nee Souders)	1873	1959
Interred in Cullen Lot.		
Gerhard, Paul D.	1895	1901
Interred in Cullen Lot.		
Gerstle, Johann	3/24/1834	8/13/1881
Gerstle, Magddalena	6/1/1835	12/10/1914
Gese, James	12/30/1904	6/24/1917
Gibbons, John	NBDR	NDDR
Buried, County Westmeath, Ireland. h/o Mary Gibbons.		
f/o Mary A., John J., & Thomas J. Gibbons.		
Gibbons, John J.	5/2/1877	12/13/1919
s/o John & Mary Gibbons.		
Gibbons, Mary A.	8/15/1867	7/31/1885
d/o John & Mary Gibbons.		
Gibbons, Mary	5/1/1840	11/30/1904
w/o John Gibbons.		
Gibbons, Thomas J.	4/3/1863	11/19/1905
s/o John & Mary Gibbons.		
Gibiruth, Job	1849	1908
Gibney, Amelia	1862	1934
Gibney, Edward F.	1858	1913
Gieringer, Andrew	11/25/1835	10/17/1902
Gieringer, Charles	1832	1906
Gieringer, M. Magdalena	12/8/1842	1/8/1882
Gieringer, Richard L.	1826	1937
Gieringer, Thomas F.	6/17/1878	11/17/1901
Gieringer, Valeria C.	9/8/1850	3/21/1920
Gieringer, William F.	10/26/1895	12/2/1900
Gierot, Agnes	1868	1946
Gierot, Stephen	1891	1958
Gierot, Valentine	1865	1923
Ginslley, Child	5/23/1863	3/18/1873
Giordan, Giuseppe	7/8/1859	9/8/1920
s/o Giuseppe & Della (nee Figli) Giordan.		

Name	Birth	Death
Giovanni, Germana	6/24/1915	7/9/1915
Giuliano, ?	5/20/1858	1/2/1930
Giuliano, Salvatore	5/15/1861	2/16/1926
Glaab, Elizabeth w/o Peter Glaab.	3/25/1821	4/12/1894
Glaab, Peter h/o Elizabeth Glaab.	NBDR	NDDR
Glaser, Conrad h/o Theresa Glaser.	3/4/1830	8/16/1892
Glaser, Theresa w/o Conrad Glaser.	2/14/1830	1/17/1909
Glaser, Maria	7/1/1900	7/1/1900
Gobel, Maria	1821	1889
Gobel, ?	8/1/1811	12/17/1886
Golden, Sister Mary Austin	NBDR	8/2/1865
Goll, Sister Mary Alonzo	NBDR	7/6/1906
Good, Andrew	1868	8/20/1910
Goreski, ? w/o Frank Goreski.	1870	1929
Goreski, Frank h/o ? Goreski.	1858	1924
Gorka, Nasza Child of Sp. & Clara Urezak.	1905	1906
Gorkes, Bernhart Born, Buchhold, Germany.	4/3/1817	11/7/1886
Gorman, Theresa (nee Sheely)	1811	2/18/1892
Goslinski, Agnes M.	1887	NDDR
Goslinski, Stanley J.	1882	1934
Graf, Annie B.	1833	1914
Graf, John	1830	1875
Grant, Andrew W.	1829	3/15/1891
Grant, Paul N. s/o John T. & Mary Grant.	2/18/1906	3/19/1906
Gratt, George (Orphan)	1862	1888
Graul, Herbert L. s/o R. & Elizabeth M Graul.	4/17/1894	12/3/1894

Name		
Greath, Catherine M. (nee Ritner)	9/18/1919	2/16/1891
w/o Samuel Greath.		
Greath, Charles E.	10/3/1857	3/9/1858
Greath, Lizzie	1837	11/25/1861
w/o Edward Greath.		
Greath, Mary C.	3/28/1856	1/20/1859
d/o Samuel & Catherine (nee Ritner) Greath.		
Greath, Samuel	6/18/1824	1/4/1869
h/o Catherine (nee Ritner) Greath.		
Greath, Sarah	8/27/1853	11/7/1854
Greath, Grace C.	1912	1976
Greely, Philip H.	1907	NDDR
Green, Catharine J.A.	3/3/1889	8/23/1908
Green, Joseph A.	1888	1965
h/o Marie A. Green.		
Green, Marie A.	1893	1921
w/o Joseph A. Green.		
Greenwalt, Ambrose	7/18/1875	11/2/1889
Gregorio, Giuseppe	1862	1904
Gregory, Alice R.	1879	1895
d/o Albert B. & Anna Gregory.		
Gregory, Albert B.	1850	1919
h/o Anna (nee Barry) Gregory.		
Gregory, Anna (nee Barry)	1852	1897
w/o Albert B. Gregory.		
Gregory, E. Genevieve	1885	1976
d/o Albert B. & Anna (nee Barry) Gregory.		
Grejtak, Anna	1866	1941
Grejtak, Jozef	1963	1/24/1916
Greth, Catharine	1/29/1814	6/8/1885
Greth, Catharine (nee Felix)	10/11/1783	11/26/1869
w/o Jacob Greth.		
Greth, Charles B.	1870	1910
Greth, David	5/15/1801	2/22/1870
Greth, David J.	8/22/1850	5/9/1899
Greth, Edward	9/5/1836	8/2/1870
Greth, Jacob	NBDR	Feb. 1816
h/o Catharine (nee Felix) Greth.		
Greth, Mary H.	NBDR	NDDR
d/o J.J. & Mary M. (nee Greer) Greth.		
Greth, Mary M. (nee Greer)	April 1852	Mar. 1911
w/o J..J. Greth.		
Greth, Rebecca aged 93 years.	NBDR	NDDR
Greth, Willied	NBDR	NDDR
s/o J. J. & Mary M. (nee Greer) Greth.		

Greth - Balbach, Caroline	1858	1889
Greth - Balbach, John	1866	1933
Greth - Balbach, Joseph	1855	1901
Grettmer, Anna	3/29/1810	4/10/1891
w/o Lorenz Grettmer.		
Grettmer, Lorenz	5/6/1816	1/7/1894
h/o Anna Grettmer.		
Grettmer, Daughter ?	11/29/1831	7/31/1900
d/o Lorenz & Anna Grettmer.		
Gretzer, Johan	7/19/1888	1/4/1890
Gretzer, Josephine	3/20/1867	9/11/1888
Gretzer, Margaretha	8/13/1850	3/3/1908
Greytok, John B.	1906	1959
Cpl 80th Troop Carrier W.W. II.		
Grieb, Christine	1850	1919
Griffith, Sarah H.	1/24/1845	9/13/1891
Grill, Emma M.	7/26/1866	5/8/1910
Grill, John	NBDR	NDDR
h/o Margaret Grill..		
Grill, John	8/4/1848	8/29/1911
Grill, Margaret	NBDR	NDDR
w/o John Grill.		
Grimm, Elizabeth	2/17/1839	8/19/1894
Grimm, John A.	1834	1913
Member of Co A 88th Regt. Pa. Volunteers Civil War.		
Griur, Cullin	6/3/1853	1/20/1927
Gross, Lewis	NBDR	NDDR
Member of Co A 73rd Pa Inf.		
Grossman, Catharine	5/20/1820	7/4/1887
Grossman, Clara R.	1864	1924
w/o Joseph Grossman.		
Grossman, Jacob	7/25/1819	10/30/1895
Grossman, Joseph Jr.	10/8/1820	12/5/1921
Grossman, Joseph	1861	1950
h/o Clara R. Grossman.		
Grossman, Joseph	7/24/1878	1/7/1911
Grossman, Kate (nee Hoch)	8/23/1856	3/5/1886
w/o Adam Grossman.		
Grossman, Mary A.	1889	1968
Grossman, Theresa	1858	1926
d/o Joseph & Clara R. Grossman.		

Gruber, Harry P.	1877	1964
Gruber, Harry J.	1905	1919
Gruber, Joseph	1829	1915
Gruber, Mary Ann (nee Deppen)	5/7/1830	5/25/1900
w/o Isaac H. Gruber.		
Gruber, Mary F.	1879	1935
Gruber, Theresia	1834	1909
Guckert, Elizabeth	1841	9/7/1882
Guenter, Adam J.	2/19/1874	12/23/1910
Guenter, John	2/15/1880	12/9/1901
Guldaman, Andrew	1817	7/13/1898
h/o Catherine Guldaman.		
Guldaman, Catherine	1824	9/22/1894
w/o Andrew Guldaman.		
Gull, Thomas	1800	NDDR
Guntner, Anna	10/16/1836	1/2/1914
w/o Franz Guntner.		
Guntner, Franz	11/26/1826	11/12/1883
h/o Anna Guntner.		
Guntner, Johanna M.	10/8/1872	4/19/1876
d/o Franz & Anna Guntner.		
Guziejewski, Antonina	1863	1927
Guziejewski, Michal	1859	1912
Guziejewski, John J.	1901	1971

- H -

Haage, Emma D.	1865	1935
Haage, George K.	1835	1906
Haage, Mary D.	1839	1913
Haage, Rosa A.	1869	1953
Haberstroh, Mary A.	1817	1907
Hackett, Dennis	1807	11/18/1883
Born, Haterford County, Ireland.		
Hackett, Mary	1817	7/2/1888
Born, Ireland.		
Haden, Konrad	9/1/1872	12/25/1890
Hadley, Catharine (nee Deemer)	3/1/1855	6/7/1900
w/o Thomas W. Hadley.		
Hadley, Edward T.	11/21/1879	11/24/1900
s/o Thomas W. & Catharine (nee Deemer) Handley.		
Hadley, Thomas W.	9/22/1855	10/28/1923
h/o Catharine (nee Deemer) Hadley.		

Name		
Hafer, Susan A.	3/24/1842	11/8/1916
Hagan, John	NBDR	NDDR
Member of Co. A 184th Inf Regt Pa Volunteers.		
Hagen, Amelia	1860	1913
Hagen, George L.	1860	1922
Haggerty, Catherine M.	1906	1906
Haggerty, Charles E.	1897	1937
Haggerty, Edward C.	1870	1941
Haggerty, Emma M.	1870	1935
Haggerty, Gertrude M. (nee Klemmer)	3/17/1882	4/8/1909
Haggerty, Kate	NBDR	NDDR
d/o William & Theresa Haggerty.		
Haggerty, Raymond C.	1911	1911
Hahn, Catharine	8/29/1785	3/18/1853
Hahn, Frances	NBDR	NDDR
Hain, Regina	1811	1908
Halbeisen, Susanna May	3/24/1918	12/26/1918
d/o Charles E. & Abbie C. Halbeisen.		
Haller, Andrew	11/16/1839	10/15/1886
Haller, Caroline	3/6/1836	2/23/1892
Haller, E.	4/16/1875	7/28/1916
Haller, Josseph B.	6/28/1873	10/6/1900
Haller, Theresa	5/22/1871	9/12/1896
Halliday, Annie E.	1872	1925
Halliday, Francis J.	1875	1948
Hankle, Christina	1831	1911
w/o George Hankle.		
Hannahoe, Andrew L.	1878	1900
Hannahoe, Barthalomew V.	1877	1901
Hannahoe, Bridget M.	1849	1932
Hannahoe, Catherine C.	1807	1893
gm/o Edward J. Hannahoe.		
Hannahoe, Edward J.	1884	1948
s/o Bridget Hannahoe.		
Hannahoe, Francis (Infant)	NBDR	NDDR
Hannahoe, Gerald	5/29/1906	12/14/1911
Hannahoe, Harry J.	1873	1892
Hannahoe, James	1839	1912
Hannahoe, James A.	1856	1926
Hannahoe, James B.	1875	1957
Hannahoe, Jane	1834	1894
Hannahoe, Margaret E.	1886	1961

Name	Birth	Death
Hannahoe, Margaret E. J.	1872	1958
Hannahoe, Mary	1859	1886
Hannahoe, Mary A.	1892	1962
Hannahoe, Michael P.	1872	1942
Hannahoe, Patrick C.	1844	1917
h/o Rosanna Hannahoe.		
Hannahoe, Peter J.	1887	1965
Cpl Hdq Detachment Transportation Corps W.W. I.		
Hannahoe, Rosanna	1847	1922
w/o Patrick C. Hannahoe.		
Hannahoe, Thomas C. (Mayor of Irishtown.)	1835	2/10/1897
Hannahoe, Thomas A.	1880	1961
Hanratty, Sister Mary Scholastica	NBDR	11/12/1868
Hantsch, Viola M.	4/12/1888	11/23/1901
Harakal, Joseph	1873	11/17/1905
Harcar, Maria	1854	3/3/1916
Harcar, Stephen	1864	9/22/1909
Harder, John	5/4/1858	8/9/1934
h/o Josephine Harder.		
Harder, Josephine	3/27/1852	10/28/1921
w/o John Harder.		
Harger, Jozef	1849	11/11/1938
Hark, Joseph	3/14/1850	2/5/1854
s/o Andreas & Eva Eleaner Hark.		
Harlow, Bridget	12/29/1849	NDDR
w/o Peter Harlow.		
Harlow, Peter	5/20/1848	5/9/1908
h/o Bridget Harlow.		
Harner, Louise	1881	1/9/1901
Orphan at St. Catharine's Orphange.		
Harrington, Bridget	1833	1907
Harrington, John	1833	1898
Harrington, Robert	1868	1884
Harrington, William	1871	1882
Hart, Mary A. (nee Bitner)	9/11/1829	12/4/1887
Hartdner, Julia (nee Rippel)	12/10/1842	7/17/1885
w/o Christian Hartdner.		
Harter, Catharine	3/31/1843	1/8/1910
Harter, John J.	1866	1937

Harter, Mary C.	1873	1910
Harter, Rosa	1897	1955
Hartman, Anna W.	1880	1951
Hartman, Barbara	1845	1912
Hartman, Johann A.	1/19/1800	10/6/1869
Hartman, Joseph	1844	1933
Hartmann, Anna Maria d/o Gottfried & Modesta Hartmann.	8/15/1868	1/23/1886
Hartmann, Gotfried h/o Modesta Hartmann.	1/22/1839	8/5/1902
Hartmann, Moldesta w/o Gottfried Hartmann.	12/15/1837	9/16/1904
Hassler, Augustus	8/28/1812	11/8/1889
Hassler, Fridolia	3/6/1805	10/1/1877
Hassler, Henrietta	1863	1921
Hassler, Rosa	1/22/1826	11/12/1874
Hasson, Ann (nee McCann) w/o James Hasson. born, Longford, Ireland.	1830	4/14/1900
Hasson, Catharine (nee Resch) w/o M. A. Hasson.	NBDR	3/22/1898
Hasson, Charles A.	1874	1936

Hasson, James
    h/o Ann (nee McCann) Hasson.
    Born, Ballinasgreen County, Londonberry, Ireland.
	1829	10/30/1891

Hasson, James J. Pvt Co E 90th Inf Regt. Civil War.	6/1/1840	12/16/1915
Hasson, John	1832	1907
Hasson, John Edward h/o Clara V. (nee Grau) Hasson.	4/22/1863	11/11/1894
Hasson, Margaret	1830	1906
Hasson, Valeria C.	1849	5/10/1907
Hauck, Emma E. w/o Wilson Hauck	2/6/1857	3/3/1883
Hauck, Martin h/o Mary Hauck	1/2/1862	3/21/1905
Hauck, Marty s/o Martin & Mary Haauck.	8/16/1891	9/19/1894
Hauck, Mary w/o Martin Hauck.	6/26/1867	1/25/1903
Haueissen, Anna E.	1868	1958
Haueissen, Charles A.	1859	1944
Hauser, Anthony s/o Michael & Barbara a. Hauser.	2/13/1859	10/19/1862
Hauser, Barbara A. w/o Michael Hauser.	11/14/1818	7/12/1903

Name	Birth	Death
Hauser, George	5/20/1856	11/24/1859
Hauser, Katie	12/21/1853	10/15/1859
d/o Michal & Barbara A. Hauser.		
Hauser, Lizzie	11/6/1858	11/6/1858
d/o Michael & Barbara A. Hauser.		
Hauer, Michael	9/7/1811	10/23/1874
h/o Barbara A. Hauser. Born in Baden, Germany.		
Heck, Mary A. (nee Becker)	1880	1948
Hegan, Dennis (Twin)	1854	5/29/1854
Hegan, Maria (Twin)	1854	5/30/1854
Children of John Hegan & Lydia Mills.		
Heilman, Carrie (nee Brice)	1903	1976
Heine, Amelia (nee Thurner)	10/7/1828	10/2/1894
Heine, Amelia S.	2/24/1883	9/18/1884
Heine, Anna M. (nee Hauck)	1890	1915
Heine, Balbina	5/17/1832	11/21/1904
Heine, Dora P. (nee Pasch)	1890	1925
Heine, Elizabeth	6/1/1868	9/17/1891
w/o Philip G. Heine.		
Heine, Gregory	2/26/1825	1/19/1914
Heine, John C.	1852	1911
Heine, Joseph	3/21/1820	8/5/1867
Born Grosshezienig, Baden, Germany.		
Heine, Joseph A.	1861	1937
Heine, Josephine	1859	1945
Heine, M. Amelia	1865	No death date.
Heine, Maria	4/1/1799	3/23/1869
w/o Philip Heine.		
Heine, Mary	7/5/1890	4/26/1893
d/o Philip G. & Elizabeth Heine.		
Heine, Mary M.	5/21/1893	3/2/1894
Heine, Philip	5/24/1786	1/?/1856
h/o Maria Heine.		
Heine, Philip G.	1/23/1830	12/25/1916
h/o Elizabeth Heine.		
Heine, Rosa A.	1863	1930
Heiniman, George	5/27/1859	8/24/1864
Heiniman, Jacob	2/12/1824	5/18/1876
h/o Susanna Heiniman.		
Heiniman, Susanna	9/22/1828	11/28/1888
w/o Jacob Heiniman.		
Heiniman, Theodore	5/3/1855	4/18/1880
Heisler, Alice	1856	1933
Heisler, Hilda	1858	1929
Heisler, Mary E.	1846	1930

Heist, Mary M. (nee Liethem) 5/27/1833 11/28/1863
    w/o Cornelius Heist. d/o Martin & Catharine Lietham.

Heizman, Carolina 1821 1855
Heizman, Charles L. NBDR NDDR

Heizman, Harry NBDR NDDR
    s/o Albert & Jennie Heizman.
Heizman, Martin 1815 1896
Heizman, Raymond L. 11/6/1879 3/26/1881
    s/o C. R. & Mary H. Heizman.

Helfrich,. Agnes L. 1908 1924
Helfrich, Annie E. 1875 1945
    w/o Henry G. Helfrich.
Helfrich, Catharine 11/11/1851 7/26/1883
Helfrich, Clara A. 1879 1917
Helfrich, Henry G. 1864 1943
    h/o Annie E. Helfrich.
Helfrich, John 6/15/1840 6/22/1902
    Member of Co C Inf Civil War. h/o Maria (nee Theornich) Helfrich.
Helfrich, John 1893 1978
Helfrich, Maria (nee Theornich) 1841 1875
    w/o John Helfrich.
Helfrich, Marie E. 7/14/1903 10/10/1918
Helfrich, Mary H. 1897 1967

Heller, Amelia M. 1842 NDDR
Heller, Francis W. 1830 1899
Heller, George H. 1872 1897

Helmstreit, Michael 2/17/1825 2/14/1883
    Born, Bavaria, Germany.

Henke, Andrew 9/14/1793 1/5/1873
    h/o Margaretta Henke.
Henke, Margaretta 2/17/1795 7/22/1868
    w/o Andrew Henke.

Henkel, Johann 4/19/1832 5/18/1874

Henrich, Anthony D. 12/6/1894 6/17/1917
    s/o Mary C. (nee Clay) Henrich.
Henrich, Anton 1/6/1834 5/29/1923
    h/o Margaretha Henrich. Born, Roschbach Rheinpfalz, Bavaria, Germany.
Henrich, E. Bernard 9/22/1903 8/4/1904
Henrich, Edward J. 8/6/1899 12/22/1903
Henrich, Jacob   aged 1-5-18 NBDR NDDR
Henrich, Johannes   aged 1-9-6 NBDR NDDR
Henrich, Margaretha 2/10/1837 9/13/1924
    w/o Anton Henrich

Henrich, Mary C. (nee Clay)	2/4/1868	10/13/1908
Mother of Anthony D. Henrich.		
Henrich, Mary M.	5/21/1893	3/2/1894
Henrich, Raymond J.	7/2/1891	8/8/1909
Henry, M.	1846	4/2/1882
Henry, William	11/12/1820	7/12/1891
Hensler, Leo	1897	1898
Hensler, Paul	1896	1896
Hensler, Samuel	1830	1907
Hensler, William b.	1861	1913
Herbein, Nicholaus	6/18/1819	NDDR
Herbst, Johannes	2/11/1822	4/7/1900
h/o Margaretha Herbst.		
Herbst, Karoline	3/29/1855	12/30/1864
d/o Johannes & Margaretha Herbst.		
Herbst, Margaretha	5/11/1822	5/22/1885
w/o Johannes Herbst.		
Herbst, Peter	5/1/1865	12/28/1891
Herm, Barbara	6/17/1844	10/10/1917
w/o John Herm.		
Herm, John	12/26/1836	2/25/1908
h/o Barbara Herm.		
Hermann, Mary (nee Bichtel)	NBDR	NDDR
Hermann, Carolina	1852	Aug. 1854
d/o Nicholaus Hermann & Elisabeth Saiher.		
Hernberger, ?	10/2/1889	11/9/1889
Hernberger, Frank	3/23/1842	7/20/1905
Hernberger, George	9/26/1879	1/3/1881
Hernberger, Greseme	5/16/1850	7/17/1911
Herrmann, Nicholas	8/5/1780	4/4/1873
Born, Saverbrigen, Bavaria, Germany.		
Hess, August	1850	1892
h/o Mary Hess.		
Hess, John B.	11/17/1849	7/4/1872
Hess, Margaret S.	4/17/1826	12/15/1900
Hess, Mary	1850	1821
w/o August Hess.		
Hesse, Patrick	NBDR	NDDR
Hill, Margaret	1851	1936
Hinnershitz, Margaretha (nee Albert)	10/ 12/1875	9/5/1899

Name	Birth	Death
Hittner, Dora L.	1878	1932
Hittner, Frank	1854	1896
Hittner, Joseph	1879	1973
Hittner, Katherine	1854	1943
Hock, Catharine	11/1/1812	9/25/1877
Hock, Margaret	12/13/1809	12/16/1873
Hodapp. John	1/20/1840	1/30/1910
h/o Mary A. (nee Mohler) Hodapp.		
Hodapp, Katharina M.	12/27/1869	3/29/1889
Hodapp, Katharine	12/31/1844	7/5/1904
w/o John F. Hodapp.		
Hodapp, Maria C.	9/11/1868	7/20/1896
Hodapp, Mary A. (nee Mohler)	1/6/1847	4/24/1875
w/o John Hodapp.		
Hodapp, Theresia	1813	9/14/1881
Hoffman, Caroline	7/2/1856	5/14/1935
Hoffman, Sarah	10/30/1854	8/11/1895
Hoffmaster, Rosalie J.	9/22/1898	12/29/1971
Hofman, Cecilia c.	2/4/1879	3/13/1886
d/o Henry & Carolina Hofman.		
Hofman, Henry	12/1/1856	3/11/1919
h/o Carolina Hofman.		
Hofman, Mary M. (nee Henigreich)	NBDR	12/20/1886
w/o Michael Hofman. Born, Nurenberg, Germany.		
Hohl, Elizabeth E.	1887	1908
Hohl, James J. Sr.	1861	1937
Hohl, Margaret C.	1863	1936
Holahan, Sister Mary A.	NBDR	3/6/1868
Holland, Catherine	1850	1916
Holland, Elizabeth (Orphan)	NBDR	11/?/1858
Holland, Kieran	1849	1913
Holland, Kieran	1/20/1884	7/16/1910
Holland, Mary E.	8/15/1885	3/11/1909
Holland, Sadie M. (nee Mayers)	1889	1956
Holland Thomas F.	10/2/1882	3/31/1909
Holland, William P,.	1881	1964
Hollywood, John A.	NBDR	NDDR
Holt, James	6/23/1908	7/19/1908
Holtzer, Anna A.	1916	1957
Hoonan, James	1863	1/21/1931

Hornicak, Andrez	5/14/1896	4/2/1917
Horvat, ?	5/29/1884	7/26/1911
Howden, Catharine A.	10/20/1840	6/17/1909
Howden, Edward	8/30/1846	7/12/1873
s/o Edward & Lovina Howden.		
Howden, Edward	1814	5/31/1890
h.o Lovina Howden. Born, County Cavan, Ireland.		
Howden, Lovina	1/3/1820	8/21/1914
w/o Edward Howden.		
Howe, James W.	2/13/1857	6/30/1896
Howe, Sarah R.	12/24/1860	3/11/1926
Huber, Mary A. (nee Bowers)	10/18/1819	6/5/1883
w/o John Huber. Born, Germany.		
Huck, Joseph F.	1854	1937
h/o Mary M. (nee Fries) Huck.		
Huck, Mary M.	1892	1964
d/o Joseph F. & Mary M. (nee Fries) Huck.		
Huck, Mary M. (nee Fries)	1855	1899
w/o Joseph F. Huck.		
Hudson, Bridget A.	1835	1910
w/o Michael Hudson.		
Huls, Bernard	8/27/1831	5/4/1917
Member Co K 54th Inf Regt Pa Volunteers, Civil War.		
h/o Hannah Huls.		
Huls, Hannah	11/14/1844	7/20/1923
w/o Bernard Huls.		
Humma, Catharine	2/21/1850	10/27/1872
Humma, Theodore	1808	1851
Huntger, Infant	NBDR	NDDR
Hunter, Emma E.	NBDR	1/23/1958
d/o Nicholas & Sophia Hunter.		
Hunter, Jacob	NBDR	3/20/1917
s/o Nicholas & sophia Hunter.		
Hunter, Sophia	NBDR	4/8/1903
w/o J Nicholas. Hunter.		
Huster, Mamie Elizabeth	4/5/1885	2/3/1888
d/o Paul & Susan Huster.		
Hutter, Henry	5/6/1831	4/20/1887
Huttner, Catharina (nee Schnetzer)	8/15/1832	6/15/1880
w/o Augustus Huttner.		

- I -

Iaeger, Catharine M.	11/29/1879	3/23/1929
Iaeger, Marguerite	7/10/1889	3/17/1892
Iaeger, Thomas K.	8/11/1925	11/21/1927
Iezzi, Adele	1868	1932
w/o Joseph Iezzi.		
Iezzi, Anna	NBDR	NDDR
Iezzi, Ike, Jr.	2/22/1928	12/10/1932
Iezzi, Joseph	1861	1935
h/o Adele Iezzi.		
Igel, Anna M.	4/28/1814	11/17/1883
Born, Prussia, Germany.		
Igel, Elisabetha	9/28/1829	3/21/1898
Igel, Nicholas (Grave marker broken cannot read.)		
Igel, Philip	9/1/1836	1/11/1925
Member of Co M 198th Inf Regt Pa Volunteers Civil War.		
Imgrund, John	9/26/18??	7/13/188?
s/o John & Louisa Imgrund.		
Imgrund, John A.	1836	1908
h/o Louisa Imgrund.		
Imgrund, Louisa	1844	1904
w/o John A. Imgrund.		
Imgrund, Theodore	2/22/18??	9/?/1882
Imlauer, Augustus	4/30/1826	7/26/1900
Imlauer, Otilia	8/21/1842	NDDR
Impink, A. Francis	4/11/1888	9/29/1888
Impink, Bernard G.H.	10/20/1827	1/24/1905
Impink, Clara	1875	1888
Impink, E. Virginia	12/10/1896	9/24/1904
Impink, George E.	12/31/1892	3/20/1893
Impink, Johan	10/17/1832	2/11/1893
Impink, Karolina (nee Ganter)	12/13/1830	10/23/1912
Impink, Lydia	1/2/1838	11/18/1905
Impink, Theresa	4/6/1873	11/5/1888
Impink, William J.	5/16/1870	3/19/1899
Ingham, Angels Stewart Nolan	NBDR	7/21/1909
w/o Thomas Hall Ingham.		
Isselburg, Cornelia	9/7/1823	9/28/1896

- J -

Jackson, Sister Mary D. 22 years of age	NBDR	2/2/18??
Jackson, Henry	12/31/1814	8/16/1896
Jackson, Maria Louisa	8/10/1825	5/2/1909
Jackson, Mary Tovey	1839	4/8/1858
Born, County Killarny, Ireland.		

Jakabein, John J.	6/16/1874	1/6/1931
Jakabein, Maria	1869	8/6/1904
Jakabein, Zofia	3/16/1873	10/27/1913
James, Mary E.	12/3/1867	7/19/1958
Jankowska, Franciszka	1901	1909
Jankowski, Amelia (nee Klempert.)	12/9/1859	1/11/1929
Jankowski, Anthony E.	NBDR	NDDR
Pa. Mech. Coast Artillery.		
Jankowski, John	6/25/1850	10/14/1946
Jankowski, Konstance	8/18/1863	11/10/1925
Jankowski, Rozalia	1850	1926
Jankowski, Tomasz	1840	NDDR
Jankowski, Wojciech	1861	1911
Januszewski, Helen L.	6/7/1900	6/9/1903
d/o Joseph & Veronika Januszewski.		
Jasinowski, Joseph	1866	1936
Jasinowski, Marie	1872	1926
Jerka, Boleslaw	NBDR	NDDR
Jerka, Jadwiga	NBDR	3/1/1954
Jerka, Ksawery	NBDR	10/11/1943
Jerka, Stephen	1896	1971
Johnson, Clara B.	10/14/1883	11/22/1950
Jones, Katherine (nee Nolan.)	NBDR	3/9/1944
d/o William Nolan.		
Jozwiak, Mich	1912	1913
Jucker, Adam	1883	1969
Jucker, Henry	1837	1887
h/o Josephine Jucker.		
Jucker, Henry	1875	1913
s/o Henry & Josephine Jucker.		
Jucker, Josephine	1848	19??
w/o Henry Jucker.		
Jucker Mary	1878	1950
d/o Henry & Josephine Jucker.		
Judge, Anna	1864	1930
Judge, John	1857	1916

- K -

Kacsur, Sister Mary D.	1893	1912

Kslbach, Benjamin E.	3/6/1834	10/23/1885
Kalbach, Catharine	8/15/1836	2/14/1920
Kalharick, Mary	1903	5/1/1904
Kalina, Anna E.	1878	1948
Kalina, John M.	1869	1948
Kamaric, Lizzie K.	1906	1907
Kaminska, ?	1851	1906
Kaminska, Vicenty	3/11/1842	5/1/1898
Kane, Ann	1819	1884
w/o Christopher Kane.		
Kane, Christopher	1802	1884
h/o Ann Kasne.		
Kane, Ellen	1882	1915
d/o James K. Kane.		
Kane, Isaac	1880	1915
s/o James K. Kane.		
Kane, James K.	1838	1930
s/o Christopher & Ann Kane.		
Kane, Marie M.	11/24/1898	9/1/1970
Kane, Thomas	1866	1900
s/o James K. Kane.		
Kaspey, Simon	4/7/1824	1/19/1892
Born, Baden, Germany.		
Kasprzewski, Walter	1893	1905
Kaufman, Maria Anna	4/9/1810	11/11/1875
w/o Michael Kaufman.		
Kaufman, Michael	1807	1877
h/o Maria Anna Kaufman.		
Kaydan, Andrew S.	11/11/1864	8/27/1951
Kaydan, Mary C.	12/7/1875	12/6/1958
Kearns, Catharine	3/22/1835	1/29/1920
Kearns, William	5/4/1831	2/14/1906
Keen, Anna C.	11/16/1900	12/27/1962
Keffer, Infant	NBDR	1886
Keffer, A.	1837	Dec. 1868
Keffer, Aaron T.C.	1829	1906
Keffer, Adam	12/24/1844	3/2/1908
Keffer, Albert	1/13/1862	8/3/1865
s/o John & Mary Keffer.		
Keffer, Anna Amanda	4/13/1842	7/1/1909
w/o Francis Keffer.		

Keffer, Bessie	2/29/1883	1/15/1884
d/o Charles A. & Ella Keffer.		
Keffer, Catharine	4/1/1868	8/23/1932
w/o Edward Keffer.		
Keffer, Charles	8/18/1860	1/10/1861
s/o John & Mary Keffer.		
Keffer, Charles	3/20/1885	7/31/1885
s/o Francis & Anna Amanda Keffer		
Keffer, Clara	1873	7/3/1912
d/o Francis & Anna Amanda Keffer.		
Keffer, Edward L.	3/27/1858	6/3/1895
h/o Catharine Keffer.		
Keffer, Emma B.	1868	1943
Keffer, Francis	1837	1919
h/o Anna Amanda Keffer.		
Keffer, Francis J.	10/4/1840	2/13/1901
Keffer, Frank	1864	1930
Keffer, Frederick	1916	1924
Keffer, Frederick C.	1879	1955
Keffer, Helen aged 3 years	NBDR	NDDR
Keffer, Henry	9/18/1844	3/15/1862
s/o John & Mary Keffer.		
Keffer, James	12/3/1818	NDDR
s/o Peter Keffer & Eliza Leveinghower.		
Keffer, J. Henry	1890	1909
Keffer, John	3/20/1816	11/19/1889
h/o Mary Keffer.		
Keffer, John	7/19/1846	3/16/1862
s/o John & Mary Keffer.		
Keffer, John	1914	1918
Keffer, Joseph F.	1874	1944
Keffer, Joseph W.	1847	1923
Keffer, Louisa Ann	11/12/1852	4/21/1891
w/o James A. Keffer.		
Keffer, Marie L.	1881	1973
Keffer, Marie L.	10/15/1889	9/5/1973
Keffer, Mary	3/20/1823	2/17/1897
w/o John Keffer		
Keffer, Mary	1/20/1852	2/23/1862
d/o John & Mary Keffer.		
Keffer, Mary B.	1857	1940
Keffer, Mary E.	1849	1930
Keffer, Michael	NBDR	3/10/1889
Keffer, Peter	6/6/1855	2/16/1862
s/o John & Mary Keffer.		
Keffer, William	1880	1919
Kehoe, Esther M.	1894	1926
Keinard, Mary E. (nee Lynch)	1893	19??
Keiser, John	12/17/1824	12/18/1892

Name	Born	Died
Keiser, ?	1827	2/9/1881
w/o John Keiser.		
Kelley, Annie E.	1847	1915
Kelley, W. M.	1848	1897
Kelly, Bernard	4/31/1843	3/31/1892
Born, Roscommon, Lacken County, Ireland.		
Kelly, Caroline (nee Greth)	5/28/1842	10/31/1907
Kelly, Carrie	9/20/1878	1/18/1903
Kelly, Frank	8/19/1866	8/20/1906
Kelly, Margaret H.	1841	1905
Kelly, Michael	1841	1911
Sgt. Co H 128th Regt. Pa. Volunteers Civil War.		
Kelly, William C.	1821	3/31/1891
Born, Ireland.		
Keltz, Helen M.	9/3/1904	9/9/1973
Keltz, John A.	7/6/1903	4/8/1972
Keltz, John T.	1875	1943
Keltz, Mary P.	1879	1934
Kemp, Clara Elizabeth	10/1/1878	10/14/1893
d/o John & Margaret Kemp.		
Kemp, Elmira Jane	3/26/1877	3/21/1885
d/o John & Margaret Kemp.		
Kemp, George	NBDR	NDDR
Kemp, George L.	NBDR	NDDR
s/o John & Margaret Kemp.		
Kemp, Ida M.	6/21/1881	9/28/1898
Kemp, Joseph	10/26/????	NDDR
Kemp, Joseph	NBDR	NDDR
h/o Justina Kemp.		
Kemp, Justina	NBDR	NDDR
w/o Joseph Kemp.		
Kemp. Margaret	7/4/1847	9/18/1916
w/o John Kemp.		
Kemp, Margaret M.	8/11/1873	10/8/1894
d/o John & Margaret Kemp.		
Kemp. Rosie Isabella	1/28/1883	2/22/1885
d/o John & Margaret Kemp.		
Kemp, Virgie	1/27/1888	12/12/1890
d/o John & Margaret Kemp.		
Kemp. Westley	NBDR	NDDR
Kern, Anna M.	1870	1888
d/o John & Maria Kern.		
Kern, John	1843	1899
h/o Maria Kern.		
Kern, Joseph	1874	1967
s/o John & Maria Kern.		
Kern, Maria	1840	1895
w/o John Kern.		

Name	Birth	Death
Kerner, A. Elizabeth	3/17/1834	3/11/1897
Born, Baltimore, Md. Died, Reading, Pa.		
Kerns, Mary	1846	3/4/1891
d/o Dennis & Mary (nee Hackett) Kerns.		
Ketterer, Catharine	8/15/1839	1/2/1867
w/o John T. Ketterer.		
Keville, Bridget	1815	2/13/1888
Keville, Patrick	1809	12/3/1884
Kieran, Sister Mary Gabriel	NBDR	8/13/1868
Klein, Caroline	12/14/1842	7/6/1895
w/o Francis Klein.		
Klein, Francis	9/23/1827	12/4/1900
h/o Caroline Klein.		
Klein, John	8/31/1835	2/1/1888
s/o Johann & Maria Klein.		
Klein, Joseph	1845	1871
s/o Johann & Maria Klein.		
Klein, Mary	7/30/1891	7/11/1892
d/o John & Anna Klein.		
Klein, Mary T.	1872	1933
Klemmer, Adam W.	1865	1936
h/o Susanna Klemmer.		
Klemmer, Annie E.	NBDR	10/4/1860
d/o Justus & Sarah A. (nee Richard) Klemmer.		
Klemmer, Benneville	5/27/1837	12/7/1916
h/o Marietta Klemmer.		
Klemmer, Caroline	10/30/1861	6/16/1889
d/o Justus & Sarah A. (nee Richard) Klemmer.		
Klemmer, Catherine	11/2/1863	4/5/1911
Klemmer, Clara G.	1872	1953
w/o George E. Klemmer.		
Klemmer, Daniel	1850	1927
Klemmer, Emma	1851	1920
Klemmer, George	4/16/1809	11/26/1893
h/o Margaret Klemmer.		
Klemmer, George E.	1867	1931
h/o Clara G. Klemmer.		
Klemmer, Gertrude	11/3/1895	5/15/1910
Klemmer, Hannah	NBDR	1/24/1891
Klemmer, Helen	8/31/1893	7/29/1894
Klemmer, Henry P.	10/2/1865	5/18/1890
s/o Justus & Sarah A. (nee Richard) Klemmer.		
Klemmer, J. Justus	5/23/1834	6/11/1894
h/o Sarah A. (nee Richard) Klemmer.		
Klemmer, Jacob	10/11/1804	4/11/1867
Klemmer, John	1798	1884

Name	Birth	Death
Klemmer, John	11/22/1859	10/29/1862
s/o Justus & Sarah A. (nee Richard) Klemmer.		
Klemmer, Leo	9/6/1900	4/10/1901
Klemmer, Loretta	3/21/1903	2/4/1920
Klemmer, Margaret	2/18/1808	5/3/1883
w/o George Klemmer.		
Klemmer, Marietta	8/18/1840	6/4/1904
w/o Benneville Klemmer.		
Klemmer, Mary	9./8/1876	8/11/1946
Klemmer, Miriam C.	11/29/1908	4/13/1911
d/o George & Clara G. Klemmer.		
Klemmer, Saforus	10/16/1840	2/12/1880
Klemmer, Sarah A. (nee Richard)	5/29/1838	1/6/1911
w/o J. Justus Klemmer.		
Klemmer, Susanna P.	1866	1951
w/o Adam W. Klemmer.		
Klemmer, William	10/1/1866	2/15/1924
Klempert, Eddie	8/16/1876	4/28/1896
Klempert, John	1874	1921
Klempert, Josephine	1885	1903
Kline, Aaron	3/7/1847	9/11/1930
Kline, Clarence	1908	1950
Kline, Daniel	1883	1913
Kline, Frank	12/11/1893	3/30/1916
Kline, Paulina M.	5/7/1848	2/10/1921
Klinikowska, Albina	11/18/1860	3/21/1910
Klinikowska, Ignacy	10/16/1879	4/30/1912
Klinikowska, Tomasz	10/16/1843	12/10/1910
Klos, Aloysius S.	12/26/1860	12/15/1905
Klos, Emma Laura	12/3/1884	3/1/1893
d/o Michael & Emma Klos.		
Klos, Henry T.	4/16/1866	2/6/1911
Klos, John S.	9/15/1857	9/8/1878
Klos, Margaret	8/8/1822	1/15/1899
Klos, Michael P.	5/13/1851	8/12/1879
Klos, Theobold	1/13/1814	5/10/1871
Klueh, Edward	1830	1920
h/o Eva Klueh.		
Klueh, Emma E.	1870	1904
Klueh, Eva	1837	1922
w/o Edward Klueh.		
Klueh, George E.	1864	1942
s/o Edward & Eva Klueh.		
Klueh, Margaret E.	1870	1932
Kluezewiez, Catharine	8/21/1821	12/30/1884
w/o Matthias Kluezewiez.		

Name	Birth	Death
Kluezewiez, Matthias h/o Catharine Kluezewiez.	9./19/1819	7/16/1906
Klump, Elizabeth w/o John Klump.	4/7/1837	12/20/1898
Klump, Elizabeth	1875	1912
Klump, George J.	1866	1945
Klump, John h/o Elizabeth Klump.	3/14/1840	1/9/1910
Klump, John	1869	1928
Klump, Mary C.	1871	1930
Klump, Rosa B.	1879	1941
Klusewitz, Andreas h/o Catharine Klusewitz.	1821	1897
Klusewitz, Anna	NBDR	NDDR
Klusewitz, August P. h/o Helen M. Klusewitz.	1895	NDDR
Klusewitz, Catharine	1821	1888
Klusewitz, Catharine V.	11/28/1890	7/9/1976
Klusewitz, Helen M. w/o Aaugust P. Klusewitz.	1899	1956
Klusewitz, John	1/16/1856	NDDR
Klusewitz, Joseph h/o Mary V. Klusewitz.	1859	1916
Klusewitz, Lorenz	8/9/1853	1/20/1928
Klusewitz, Louisa	2/11/1862	12/11/1940
Klusewitz, Mary V. w/o Joseph Klusewitz.	1859	1947
Klusewitz, Michael	NBDR	NDDR
Klusewitz, Stanislaw S. Corporal Troop K 11th Cavalry U.S. Army W.W. I.	5/8/1895	5/9/1918
Klusewitz, Victoria M.	12/25/1860	NDDR
Knapp, August s/o George & Margaret Knapp.	3//13/1863	1866
Knapp, George h/o Margaret Knapp.	11/22/1822	2/22/1864
Knapp, George s/o George & Margaret Knapp.	12/18/1847	5/20/1904
Knapp, Margaret w/o George Knapp.	2/19/1823	6/25/1898
Knochel, Caroline Born in Philadelphia, Pa. d/o Frank & Katharina Knochel.	12/26/1847	6/15/1864
Knochel, Frank h/o Katharina Knochel.	1814	1885
Knochel, Katharina w/o Frank Knochel.	1817	1886
Kobel, Catherine	1848	1867

Name	Birth	Death
Kober, Ellen L.	1859	1939
Kober, George M.	1863	1940
Kobilak, Andrew	1902	1938
Koch, A. Mary	1830	6/7/1896
Koch, Anna L. (nee Kohler)	4/23/1890	5/4/1959
Koch, Emma	1853	1926
Koch, Isaac	1841	1913
Koch, John George	3/20/1864	11/28/1906
Kochan, Tomasz	1863	1908
Koenig, Andrew	11/22/1826	4 /30/1917
Koenig, Anton	10/21/1821	6/27/1887
Koenig, George	2/12/1800	9/9/1882
Koenig, Elizabeth (nee Ebling)	NBDR	NDDR
Koenig, Francis	7/17/1858	9/28/1872
Koenig, Josepha	11/19/1823	4/22/1889
Koenig, Mary	8/17/1856	6/10/1852
Koenig, Mary Anna	5/13/1831	12/19/1872
Koenig, William	NBDR	NDDR

Kohler, A. Charles   6/7/1864   3/24/1930
     s/o Bernhard & Theresa Kohler. h/o Anna A. Kohler.

Kohler, Anna A.   10/18/1867   6/19/1922
     w/o A. Charles Kohler.

Kohler, August   10/20/1877   4/24/1900
     s/o Bernhard & Theresa Kohler.

Kohler, Bernhard   11/11/1835   12/17/1896
     h/o Theresa Kohler.

Kohler, Clara (nee Lichty)   2/28/1892   4/17/1931

Kohler, Edward   1/15/1875   8/30/1898
     s/o Bernhard & Theresa Kohler.

Kohler, Edward A.   2/17/1902   12/30/1963

Kohler, George L.   3/6/1891   3/15/1945
     Pvt 26th Inf Div W.W. II.

Kohler, Helen   1900   1973
Kohler, Michael P.   1890   1949
Kohler, Theresa   5/24/1841   5/30/1921
     w/o Berhard Kohler.

Kolina, Adam	NBDR	1/10/1919
Konig, Adam	5/29/1832	12/17/1876
Korb, Anna Maria	1810	1872
Korb, Anton	1819	1883
Korb, Sabina	1827	1895
Korejivo, Theodora M. (nee Zawidski)	1869	1898
Korejivo, ?	3/25/1868	4/25/1903

Kormana, Clara	5/8/1880	9/11/1935
Kornacki, Stanislaw	1842	1886
Kostival, Michael	10/15/1898	7/15/1900
Kozlowski, Anastazya	1871	1918
Kozlowski, Antoni	1868	1950
Kozlowski, Elizabeth J.	1899	1974
Kozlowski, Joseph F.	1904	NDDR
Kraemer, Theodore	1900	1901
Kraemer, Theresa	9/27/1866	6/26/1941
Krafft, Catharine	2/25/1841	3/2/1911
Krafft, Nicholas	11/18/1837	4/1/1896
Kramer, Andrew	7/23/1851	8/27/1896
Kramer, Anna	4/12/1829	NDDR
Kramer, Balbina	10/23/1840	10/19/1896
Kramer, George	6/16/1843	3/6/1891
Member of Co C 8th Pa. Cavalry, Civil War.		
Kramer, Ignatus	5/16/1903	4/10/1931
Kramer, Joseph	12/27/1839	2/1/1911
Kramp, Thomas J.	12/8/1901	9/19/1918
Kremp, Carolyn M. (nee Prestat)	7/2/1823	4/2/1883
w/o Louis Kremp.		
Kremp, Dominic	6/13/1832	1/3/1914
Kremp, Elizabeth	7/19/1800	5/9/1871
Kremp, Joseph P.	NBDR	10/31/1902
h/o Laura A. (nee Miller) Kremp.		
Kremp, Laura A. (nee Miller)	NBDR	1/4/1939
w/o Joseph P. Kremer.		
Kremp, Louis	10/26/1820	3/15/1898
h/o Carolyn M. (nee Prestat) Kremp		
Kremp, Matilda Only date on marker is October 3rd. No year given.		
Kremp, Xavier	4/13/1791	4/13/1857
Krempasanka, Mihal	9/20/1864	2/2/1917
Krempaski, Andrew J.	1909	1977
Krempaski, Antoinette	1912	NDDR
Kreth, Daniel	3/12/1803	9/20/1856
Kriebiehler, Gertrude	2/28/1836	1/20/1912
w/o Sebastian Kriebiehler.		
Kriebiehler, Magdalena	10/21/1871	10/30/1899
Kriebiehler, Sebastian	11/5/1822	1/26/1902
h/o Gertrude Kriebiehler.		

Name		
Krivi, Mary	1892	1928
w/o Paul A. Krivi.		
Krivi, Paul A.	1894	1952
h/o Mary Krivi.		
Kroener, Freddie J.	7/12/1893	5/4/1895
Kroener, Robbie	2/14/1892	5/31/1893
Krug, Anna F.	10/31/1834	1/26/1901
Krug, Lousia	8/22/1872	2/19/1876
Krug, Michael	1/16/1829	7/9/1903
Krug, Rose (nee Auer)	12/29/1873	10/6/1895
w/o Augustus J. Krug.		
Kruppenbacher, Amelia	NBDR	NDDR
w/o John A. Kruppenbacher.		
Kruppenbacher, John A.	NBDR	7/26/1900
h/o Amelia Kruppenbacher.		
Krzyzanowski, George	1879	1955
Krzyzanowski, Katharine	1885	1978
Krzyzanowski, Theodore	1911	NDDR
Krzyzanowski, William	1918	1963
Kubacki, Antonina	1858	1911
Kubacki, Richard D.	1927	1981
Kubacki, Stanislaw	1849	1913
Kube, Helena	10/22/1889	3/21/1890
d/o Albert & Maria Kube.		
Kuhn, Juliana	1801	3/6/1878
w/o Adam Kuhn.		
Kuhns, Elizabeth	2/20/1823	10/18/1898
Kuhns, Frank	1868	1938
h/o Katherine Kuhns.		
Kuhns, Hannah	1856	1922
w/o James H. Kuhns.		
Kuhns, Henry	4/3/1826	5/9/1898
Kuhns, Henry K.	2/6/1864	5/26/1916
Kuhns, James H.	1854	1944
h/o Hannah Kuhns.		
Kuhns, John H.	1882	1938
Kuhns, Katherine	1867	1924
we/o Frank Kuhns.		
Kuhns, Mable E.	1/10/1884	7/24/1886
d/o Ambrose & Lucy Kuhns.		
Kuly, Miklus	8/1/1914	9/25/1915
Kurczewski, Andrew	1851	5/24/1927
Kurczewski, Elizabeth	1858	5/1/1921

Kurfess, Franz A.   10/27/1840   10/11/1915
    h/o Matilda Kurfess. Born, Neuhauser, Wurttemberg. Germany.
Kurfess, Matilda   3/1/1846   NDDR
    w/o Franz A. Kurfess. born Darmstadt, Hessen, Germany.

Kutigier, Maria A. (nee Rothmund)   1/10/1820   3/5/1872
    w/o Joseph Kutigier.

Kwiatkowski, Antoni   1861   1926
Kwiatkowski, Mary Anna   1871   1915

- L -

Labe, John I.   1/11/1889   5/15/1918

Lafata,. Vincenzo   1871   1/25/1908
    s/o Michele & Francesca Ropella Lafata.
    Born, Belmente Missagno Pro. Palermo, Italy.

Lamanna, Frank A.   1888   1909
Lamanna, Jerome A.   1893   1900

Lamanna, Luigi   1853   1931
Lamanna, Rafalla M.   1856   1905
Lamanna, Vincenzo P.   1881   1902

Lambert, Margaret   7/27/1806   12/29/1868
    d/o Josseph & Anna Margaret Allgaier.

Lamonica, Carmela   1889   2/3/1915
Lamonica, Joseph   12/3/1913   12/26/1927
Lamonica, Lucia   8/7/1853   7/25/1926
Lamonica, Rosario   1885   1915

Landtwing, ?   1863   7/25/1905
Landtwing, Xavier   1849   7/5/1900
    Member of Co F 6th Inf Regt Civil War.

Langore, Matteo   1864   1911
    h/o Colombina Langore.
Langore, Colombina   1866   1910
    w/o Matteo Langore.

LaPenna, Lorgetrix   5/20/1900   4/20/1908
    d/o Nigola & Libaria LaPenna.

Lappan, Sister Mary Teresa   NBDR   10/28/1865

Larkin, Barbara A.   1858   1945
Larkin, Edward S.   NBDR   2/7/1899
Larkin, John F. Sr.   1828   1904
Larkin, Mary A.   1840   1904
Larkin, Michael A.   1858   1889

Name	Birth	Death
Lauter, Catharine w/o Gerhard Lauter.	1834	1887
Lauter, Francis (aged 13 years) s/o Gerhard & Catharine Lauter.	NBDR	NDDR
Lauter, Gerhard h/o Catharine Lauter.	1829	1916
Lauther, Charles	1835	1913
Lauther, Elizabeth	1841	1911
Lavy, ?	2/15/1859	3/6/1924
Lavy, Edward L.	2/14/1889	7/28/1910
Lavy, Mary E.	10/31/1866	11/29/1929
Lawrence, John L.	6/22/1831	2/3/1905
Leabeck, Mary d/o Nicholas & Margaret Leabeck.	May 1850	Sept 1873
Leabeck, Margaret w/o Nicholas Leabeck.	July 1822	April 1876
Leabeck, Nicholas h/o Margaret Leabeck.	Jan 1826	June 1880
Lee, Emma	7/6/1853	12/22/1894
Leilghtam, ? Member of Co G 9th Regt Pa Volunteer's. Spanish American War	1873	1923
Leisz, Benedict	NBDR	12/23/1888
Leisz, Elizabeth	NBDR	2/16/1900
Leitham, Catharine w/o Martin Leitham.	12/15/1801	12/7/1878
Leitham, Martin h/o Catharine Leitham.	3/15/1800	10/31/1880
Lembo, Carmello	10/14/1914	11/30/1915
Lemmer, ?	NBDR	NDDR
Lemmer, George J. h/o Masbel L. (nee Stamm) Lemmer.	1883	1938
Lemmer, Mabel L. (nee Stamm) w/o George J. Lemmer.	1891	1914
Lemon, Henry Aged 57 years.	1795	8/?/1852
Lemon, Martin	1814	1866
Lemon, Matilda	1817	1901
Lentgraf, Anna w/o Kasper Lentgraf.	5/24/1842	12/19/1904
Lentgraf, Ida d/o Kasper & Anna Lentgraf.	1/1/1883	9/16/1910

Lentgraf, Kasper	9/8/1840	11/11/1919
h/o Anna Lentgraf.		
Lentgraf, Margaret	5/5/1836	1/31/1923
w/o Michael Lentgraf.		
Lentgraf, Michael	12/25/1842	12/17/1912
h/o Margaret Lentgraf.		
Leonardziak, Frances	1885	1921
Leonardziak, Frank	1877	1942
Leone, Raffaefa	1843	1927
Lesagonicz, Anna	1918	1920
Lesko, Stephen	8/27/1872	2/17/1916
Lewandowska, Mae	1850	1909
Lewandowska, Stanley	1861	1942
Lewicki, Anna M.	1868	1929
Lewicki, Antoni J.	NBDR	1909
Lewicki, Joseph F.	1895	1965
Lewicki, Michael	1855	1913
Leydy, Rudolf	NBDR	NDDR
Liebeck, ?	2/25/1825	8/7/1875
Liebeck, George	7/7/1824	10/19/1880
Liederer, Joachin	3/21/1813	3/7/1888
Liederer, Margaretha	NBDR	NDDR
iesman, Clara C.	1879	1958
Liesman, Joseph	9/24/1819	7/17/1894
Liesman, Joseph F.	1878	1917
Liesman, ?	1/2/1862	12/5/1873
Liesman, Gertrud	5/24/1825	12/21/1900
Liesman, J. Elizabeth	2/3/1863	6/19/1872
Lill, Frank	12/21/1830	5/14/1911
h/o Margaretha Lill.		
Lill, Margaretha	8/22/1830	7/22/1877
w/o Frank Lill.		
Lillis, John V.	1882	3/7/1914
s/o Thomas J. & Mary M. Lillis.		
Lillis, Mary M.	1850	11/25/1911
w/o Thomas J. Lillis.		
Lillis, Thomas J.	1848	11/25/1911
h/o Mary M. Lillis.		
Ling, Sister Mary Felicitas	3/7/1872	NDDR

Lingel, Amanda E.	1835	5/5/1888
Lingel, Catharine B.	3/9/1860	9/18/1896
w/o David J. Lingel.		
Lingel, David J.	1828	4/26/1876
h/o Catharine B. Lingel.		

- M -

Maciejewski, Ella V.	1889	1952
Maciejewski, Martin	1886	1954
Member of 13th Field Artillery. W.W. I.		
Mack, Frank C.	12/21/1877	9/21/1879
Mackowiak, Jad	NBDR	NDDR
Mackowiak, T.	NBDR	NDDR
Mackowiak, Tom	NBDR	1873
Madary, Catharine	NBDR	3/22/1871
Benefactress of Orphans.		
Madeira, Florence	1891	1931
Maher, Annie Aged 7 years.	NBDR	NDDR
gd/o Martin & Matilda Lemon.		
Mahoney,. Mary	4/25/1855	3/24/1890
Maier, F.	1787	1810
Maier, Johan	1811	1882
Maimone, Antonio	1844	10/15/1908
Malinowski, Franciszek	1880	1964
Malinowski, Stanislawa	5/5/1853	12/2/1921
Malinowski, Wojciech	4/2/1849	3/21/1916
Malinowski, Rosalia	1883	1956
Mallehan, Patrick	1818	NDDR
Malzona, Joseph	2/26/1889	5/28/1896
Mancuso, Vincenzo	1889	8/22/1911
Maniaci, Anthony	2/24/1876	5/13/1935
h/o Louise Maniaci.		
Maniaci, Loulise	9/20/1887	11/17/1964
w/o Anthony Maniaci.		
Maniaci, Maria	9/27/1905	7/3/1913
d/o Anthony & Louise Maniaci.		
Marcincin, Anna (nee Kollar)	1862	1930
w/o Mathias Marcincin.		

Name		
Marcincin, Mathias	3/19/1856	7/21/1830
h/o Anna (nee Kollar) Marcincin.		
Marinic, Cyula	4/6/1890	10/5/1906
Marinitz, Elizabeth	1886	1909
Marinitz, Joseph	1845	1998
Marinitz, Margaret	1908	1909
Marinitz, Matilda	1850	1927
Marinitz, Stephen	1893	1935
Markert, George	5/24/1811	7/25/1899
Born, Klossterhausen, Bavaria, Germany.		
Marquart, Joseph	3/25/1857	11/22/1897
Marquart, Margaret	10/5/1843	8/12/1910
Marquart, Martin	11/26/1834	11/5/1898
Marquart, Mary A.	10/31/1824	3/30/1905
Marquart, Theresa	8/25/1875	10/20/1918
Marongelle, Rocco	1871	1917
Martin, Joseph	1815	7/13/1881
Martin, Mother Mary Magdalena	NBDR	12/4/1866
Marullo, Antonia	10/8/1916	6/27/1917
Marullo, Orlando Margarita	5/18/1886	1/21/1913
Masek, Sister Amalia	1855	1920
Maserak, W.	NBDR	NDDR
Mattick, Robert F.	7/11/1922	11/21/1927
Mauer, Katharina	1873	3/25/1907
Maurer, Annie	1815	1885
Maurer, Fortunatus	1811	1886
Maurer, Henrietta	1850	1936
Maurer, John	1851	1933
Maurer, Kathryn R.	1866	1937
Maurer, William	1875	1877
Mayer, Marcus	1823	1878
Mayer, Matilda	8/5/1849	6/28/1884
Mazza, Maria	1865	1930
Mazza, Pasquale	1861	1911
McCaffrey, ?	1804	1879
Born, County Caven, Ireland.		
Mcaffrey, James	1853	10/8/1897

McCann, Bessie   10/20/1882   2/11/1883
    d/o John & Bridget C. McCann.
McCann, Bridget C.   6/29/1853   3/8/1924
    w/o John McCann.

McCann, Catharine   NBDR   1872
    Born, Cavan Parish, Killmore, Ireland.
McCann, Dora G.   1890   1975
McCann, Edward   NBDR   8/8/1945
    Born, Cavan Parish, Killmore, Ireland.
McCann, Edward J.   1880   1963
    h/o Margaret V. (nee DeVine) McCann.
McCann, Ellen M.   1889   1968
McCann, Ellie   1/31/1860   5/31/1876
McCann, John   10/15/1847   4/6/1895
    h/o Bridget McCann.
McCann, Katie   9/20/1877   4/17/1883
    d/o John & Bridget McCann.
McCann, Margaret V. (nee DeVine)   1882   1909
    w/o Edward J. McCann.
McCann, Mary X.   3/10/1884   1/17/1938
    d/o John & Bridget McCann.
McCann, Michael   1815   2/18/1881
    Born, County Lonford, Cornish Parish, Ireland.
McCann, Rosie   1884   6/18/1897
    St. Catharine's Orphan Asylum.
McCann, Veronica M.   1909   1921
    d/o Edward J. & Margaret V. (nee DeVine) McCann.
McCann, William Leo   9/10/1875   3/20/1885
    s/o John & Bridget McCann.

McCarthy, Mary (nee Eckenroad)   1856   1911
    w/o William McCarthy.
McCarthy, William   1851   NDDR
    h/o Mary McCarthy.

McCauley, Margaret J. (nee Cooney)   1897   1963

McClosky, Catharine   11/1/1832   8/1/1908
McClosky, Henry   1/15/1822   12/29/1891
    Born, County Derry, Ireland.

McCollough, Catharine   1844   8/30/1903
    Born, County Tyrone, Ireland. w/o James McCollough.
McCollough, Michael   10/5/1868   12/24/1876

McConkey, Edward   12/25/1816   4/2/1884
    Born, County Antrim, Ireland.
McConkey, Edward F.   9/6/1852   10/7/1927
    Born in Ireland. h/o Isabella McConkey.
McConkey, John   5/31/1857   7/29/1923
McConkey, John J.   2/10/1887   3/10/1893

| McConkey, Isabella | 3/7/1850 | 12/28/1920 |

w/o Edward F. McConkey. Born in Ireland.

McConnell, Ellen aged 6 years.	NBDR	NDDR
McConnell, Ellen	1852	5/15/1922
McConnell, Margaret aged 4 years.	NBDR	NDDR
McConnell, Patrick	1843	3/10/1902
McConnell, Rose	1871	6/22/1958

| McCullough, ? | 1857 | 12/22/1892 |

Born, Badany Parish, County Tyrone, Ireland.

| McCullough, Angel | 1932 | 1932 |
| McCullough, Bernard A. | NBDR | 10/19/1925 |

Member Co B 128th Inf. Pa Volunteer's Civil War.

| McCullough, Catharine | 1817 | 9/11/1891 |

w/o Daniel McCullough.
Born, Badany Parish, County Tyrone, Ireland.

| McCullough, Cecelia | 1888 | 1960 |
| McCullough, Daniel | 1807 | 10/15/1890 |

h/o Catharine McCollough.
Born, Badany Parish, County Tyrone, Ireland.

| McCullough, Daniel E. | 10/8/1867 | 4/9/1885 |

s/o Michael & Margaret McCullough.

| McCullough, Daniel M. | 11/12/1874 | 7/21/1895 |
| McCullough, Edward | 8/18/1828 | 3/30/1871 |

Born, County Cavan, Ireland.

McCullough, Edward J.	1874	1943
McCullough, Francis	1800	1883
McCullough, Francis J.	12/15/1845	8/16/1916
McCullough, Frank	1849	11/26/1914

Born, County Tyrone, Ireland.

| McCullough, James | 1833 | 1/31/1914 |

Born, County Tyrone, Ireland.

McCullough, Joseph	1876	2/29/1924
McCullough, Joseph I.	1909	7/7/1909
McCullough, Margaret	1837	3/21/1892

w/o Michael McCullough.

McCullough, Margaret E.	1903	1980
McCullough, Mary	12/31/1845	2/9/1906
McCullough Michael	1834	9/12/1899

h/o Margaret McCullough.
Born, County Tyrone, Ireland.

McCullough, Paul J.	1900	3/1/1915
McCullough, Rose T.	1878	8/10/1951
McCullough, Susan aged 70 years.	NBDR	NDDR

Born, Badany Parish, County Tyrone, Ireland.

| McDarby, Bernard | 1826 | 1908 |

h/o Mary(nee Quinn) McDarby.

| McDarby, Mary (nee Quinn) | 1830 | 1890 |

w/o Bernard McDarby.

| McDarby, Margret J. | 1873 | 1947 |

McDermott, James	3/9/1861	12/26/1885
McDermott, Mary	1829	4/19/1899
McDermott, Peter	1827	1/27/1879
McDevitt, John	1804	12/5/1858
McDevitt, John H.	12/16/1854	11/19/1909
McDevitt, Margaret	1808	7/29/1884
McDevitt, Mary	10/30/1854	10/10/1899
McDonald, Mary	1833	4/4/1916
McDonald, William	1834	7/5/1901
McDonell, Catharine	1831	11/7/1895
w/o Francis McDonell.		
McDonell, Ellen C.	1865	1956
McDonell, Francis`	1829	2/28/1907
h/o Catharine McDonell.		
McDonell, Francis	1866	1936
McDonell, Mary J.	1857	1941
McDonough Dr. A. A.	NBDR	4/13/1869
McDonough, Bartholmew	1828	10/8/1974
Born, Killian, County Galway, Ireland.		
Died, South Orange, N.J.		
McDonough, Catharine A.	NBDR	10/26/1923
w/o William P. Mcdonough.		
McDonough, Charles M.D.	7/7/1886	5/5/1962
McDonough, John	NBDR	2/15/1913
McDonough, Matilda	1838	1921
McDonough, William P.	NBDR	2/23/1932
h/o Catharine A. McDonough.		
McDonough, Winifred	NBDR	8/1/1889
McElhone, Sister Mary Cecilia	NBDR	3/30/1862
McEvoy, Ann	NBDR	8/22/1903
w/o James McEvoy.		
McEvoy, Annie C.	NBDR	8/8/1901
McEvoy, James	NBDR	8/26/1917
h/o Ann Evoy.		
McEvoy, John	NBDR	12/31/1913
s/o James & Ann McEvoy.		
McEvoy, Margaret M.	NBDR	6/6/1961
McEvoy, Mary C.	NBDR	11/25/1961
McEvoy, William	NBDR	10/23/1906
McGariety, ?	NBDR	10/14/1896
McGee, Daniel	1/7/1827	9/7/1902
McGee, Ellen,	1821	1/2/1896
McGee, John F.	7/22/1854	10/4/1925
Mcgee, Margaret	4/11/1851	1/28/1886

McGinley, James	1846	12/31/1904
McGinley, Stephen	NBDR	9/9/1914
Born, Tyrone County, Ireland.		
McGinley, Susan	NBDR	5/1/1915
Born, Tyrone County, Ireland.		
McGlinchey, Sarah	3/25/1830	4/9/1922
Born, Convoy, Donegal County, Ireland.		
McGlinchey, Mary	8/4/1835	1/31/1916
Born, Convoy, Donegal County, Ireland.		
McGlone, Mary	1880	1959
Buried, William Morris lot.		
McGovern, A. Marie	1911	1912
McGovern, Catharine	8/13/1885	4/22/1917
McGovern, Francis X.	1880	1925
McGovern, James	1917	1918
McGovern, Margaret	1857	2/26/1890
McGovern, Mary C.	1885	1918
McGovern, Mary F.	1850	11/22/1913
McGovern, Patrick	1805	11/25/1872
McMenamin, Catherine	1874	1916
McNamee, Annie	9/15/1887	4/15/1889
McNamee, Francis	1830	10/8/1876
Born, Badon Parish, County Tyrone, Ireland.		
Mealey, Catharine	11/18/1839	3/16/1908
Mealey, Patrick	8/28/1840	8/18/1908
Meisen, Anthony	8/21/1875	12/5/1908
Menges, Monika	5/24/1824	4/5/1907
Meo, Antonio	1873	7/21/1912
Merges, Anna H.	10/12/1810	4/16/1894
w/o Nicholas Merges.		
Merges, Nicholas	1/10/1814	12/10/1891
h/o Anna H. Merges.		
Merget, Emilie Helene	4/26/1855	8/4/1859
Merget, Jacob	4/15/1814	11/18/1891
h/o Magdalena Merget.		
Merget, Joseph	11/2/1857	8/12/1859
Merget, Louis J.	5/1/1853	6/28/1893
Merget, Magdalena	5/4/1821	1/27/1897
w/o Jacob Merget.		
Merkel, Henry	1870	1928
Merkel, Justine (nee Leitz)	5/22/1822	2/9/1900

Name		
Merkel, Rudolph	1854	6/29/1854
s/o Simon Merkel & Juztine Leitz.		
Merkel, Simon	3/13/1820	9/19/1893
h/o Justine (nee Leitz) Merkel.		
Messmer, Andrew	11/10/1827	6/14/1896
Messmer, Theresa	10/24/1838	3/4/1913
Messner, Elizabeth	9/3/1846	6/19/1882
Messner, John	5/12/1843	11/24/1893
Metinier, Charles J.	1875	1927
Michael, Amelia	6/19/1848	10/3/1913
Michael, Jacob C.	2/5/1848	5/10/1906
Michalik, John	3/19/1911	8/19/1912
Mickewicz, Enmelia	1870	1940
Mickewicz, Maria (nee Kemper)	NBDR	8/16/1923
Mickewicz, Josdeph Peteer	1854	1906
Miglionico, Joseph	NBDR	NDDR
Mihaly, Mary	NBDR	NDDR
Mikolajczak, Bernice C.	1903	NDDR
Mikolajczak, Eugene D.	1930	NDDR
Mikolajczak, Joseph F.	1900	1968
Milaniak, Katarine E.	11/21/1906	6/1/1941
Miller, Amanda	1861	1916
Miller, Amelia	1867	1907
Miller, Annie	1869	1944
Miller, Catharine	8/24/1830	7/25/1895
Miller, Ella E. (nee Case)	1872	1909
w/o Howard R. Miller.		
Miller, Falicita K.	12/25/1845	1/13/1891
w/o William S. Miller.		
Miller, Henry	1825	1906
Miller, Howard R.	1874	1900
h/o Ella E. (nee Case) Miller. s/o J. Russell & Emily Miller.		
Miller, Isabella (nee St. Clair)	12/1/1813	12/11/1872
w/o Valentine Miller.		
Miller, Jacob	5/27/1857	10/2/1890
Miller, Philip	4/27/1828	6/8/1895
Miller, Philip C. Jr.	1865	1906
Minicozzi, Antoni	1931	1935
Miraabella, Rosa	1889	1922

Miscorewicz, Agnieszka	1875	1949
Miscorewicz Boleslaw	1878	1937
Miscorewicz, Stanislaw	1912	1912
Mislinski, Jon	1890	1918
Mitchell, Joseph S.	7/10/1891	3/8/1978
Pvt Co A U.S. Army Engr W.W. I.		
Moll, Gerhard	9/21/1832	5/16/1898
Moll, Gertrude	6/2/1826	10/2/1885
w/o Richard Moll.		
Mollica, Antonina	1879	1942
w/o Salvatore Mollica.		
Mollica, Joseph	1886	1966
Mollica, Phillip	1916	1977
Mollica, Salvatore	1874	1951
h/o Antonina Mollica.		
Mollica, Samuel	10/18/1918	11/3/1918
s/o Joseph & Mary Mollica.		
Mollica, Samuel	1925	NDDR
Mollica, Tindara	1894	1967
Mooney, Genesis	1853	7/19/1854
s/o John Mooney & Maria Wilkson.		
Moore, Bridget L.	1866	1933
Moore, Clara H.	1854	1922
Moore, William J.	3/23/1891	1/15/1907
Moran, Anna	1812	1881
Morris, Andrew B.	2/6/1878	1/24/1915
Morris, Anna Mae	1912	NDDR
Morris, Annie A. (nee Seidel)	1881	1953
Morris, Anna B.	NBDR	2/4/1960
Morris, Bernard	1906	1972
Morris, Bridget	NBDR	10/24/1916
w/o Patrick Morris.		
Morris, Charles E.	NBDR	3/31/1948
Morris, Edward P.	NBDR	11/3/1903
Morris, Edward S.	NBDR	9/11/1941
Morris, Jennie P.	NBDR	1/6/1947
d/o Patrick & Bridget Morris.		
Morris, Joan Ann	NBDR	1940
Morris, John W.	5/19/1879	1/5/1946
Morris, Magdalena (nee Klemmer)	NBDR	12/12/1908
Morris, Margaret C.	11/30/1878	5/9/1917
Morris, Marie C.	7/28/1892	10/6/1913
d/o Simon & Sarah Morris.		
Morris, Martha	1853	1925
w/o William J. Morris.		

Morris, Mary A.	NBDR	3/9/1932
Morris, Nora	NBDR	1904
St. Catharine's Orphan Asylum.		
Morris, Patrick	NBDR	10/18/1910
h/o Bridget Morris.		
Morris, Paul J.	NBDR	8/16/1953
s/o Patrick & Bridget Morris.		
Morris, Rose	1884	1969
Morris, Sadie C.	NBDR	2/12/1917
Morris, Sarah	NBDR	3/6/1924
w/o Simon Morris.		
Morris, Simon	NBDR	2/21/1933
h/o Sarah Morris.		
Morris, William J.	1852	1922
h/o Martha Morris.		
Morris William J.	1886	1960
Morrissey, John	12/10/1881	7/11/1882
Moyer, Emma	1/16/1847	8/21/1914
w/o Samuel E. Moyer.		
Moyer, George W.	2/19/1891	12/2/1906
Moyer, Lizzie	1/11/1862	9/16/1890
w/o Marion Moyer.		
Moyer, Samuel E.	1883	1916
Mullet, Annie E. (nee Flood)	NBDR	1/16/1928
Mullet, John f.	NBDR	1/29/1913
Mullet, Thomas	1844	1/22/1873
Born, Ballendager Parish, Wexford County, Ireland.		
Murphy, Bridget	1840	1910
Murphy, Bridget V.	1865	1949
w/o Patrick Murphy.		
Murphy, Joseph P.	6/18/1898	8/13/1927
Murphy, Patrick J.	1866	1956
h/o Bridget V. Murphy.		
Murr, Anthony	1/17/1858	1/1/1911
Murr, Wilhelmina	6/29/1870	4/2/1924
Murray, Annie A.	NBDR	NDDR
Murray, Catharine A. (nee Harrington)	1863	1898
Murray, Catharine C.	NBDR	NDDR
Murray, John	1834	8/3/1916
h/o Susan Murray.		
Murray, Margaret C.	NBDR	NDDR
Murray, Mary	NBDR	4/11/1950
Murray, Peter J.	NBDR	1907
Murray, Susan	1839	8/13/1914
w/o John Murray.		

Murry, James	NBDR	1898
h/o Mary Murry.		
Murry, Mary	NBDR	1908
w/o James Murry.		
Murry, James J.	NBDR	1927
s/o of James & Mary Murry.		
Myles, C. Alberta (nee Deppen)	1886	1950

- N -

Ninfo, Maria (nee Santospereto)	3/7/1901	1925
w/o Sebastian Ninfo.		
Nistle, Barbara	12/14/1825	4/14/1897
Nistle, George	3/20/1871	6/12/1925
Nistle, Sabastian	10/16/1829	1/18/1913
Nitarki, Frances	1894	1920
Nolan, Ann (nee Bennett)	1794	1/23/1892
Born, Roundwood, Ireland.		
Nolan, Charles	4/8/1838	4/6/1908
Nolan, Charles	1838	2/10/1891
Born, Ireland.		
Nolan, Charles T.	11/10/1877	9/29/1909
s/o Thomas & Helen Nolan.		
Nolan, Edward J.	2/18/1846	1/9/1890
Born, Clonaslee, Queen County, Ireland.		
h/o Mary (nee Liederer) Nolan.		
Nolan, F. Reilly	10/5/1883	6/2/1914
Nolan, Gerada	NBDR	NDDR
Infant s/o Thomas & Helen Nolan.		
Nolan, Helen T.	NBDR	6/12/1918
w/o Thomas Nolan.		
Nolan, James	1/9/1844`	NDDR
Nolan, James B.	12/1/1872	4/10/1923
Nolan, Katherine	1849	5/15/1897
w/o William Nolan.		
Nolan, Katie (nee Stewart)	NBDR	NDDR
w/o James Nolan.		
Nolan, Margaret C.	12/20/1874	6/7/1931
Nolan, Mary	NBDR	NDDR
Infant d/o Thomas & Helen Nolan.		
Nolan, Mary (nee Liederer)	2/2/1855	2/2/1889
w/o Edward J. Nolan.		
Nolan, Patrick	NBDR	NDDR
Infant s/o Thomas & Helen Nolan.		
Nolan, Thomas	7/4/1843	11/30/1892
Born, Clonaslee, Queen County, Ireland. h/o Helen T. Nolan.		
Nolan,, William, Jr	1840	2/28/1903
Nolan, William M.	4/16/1879	6/13/1916
s/o Thomas & Helen Nolan.		

Name	NBDR	NDDR
Nolzah-e?, Andrew Member of Co K.	NBDR	NDDR
Noonan, Emma	7/29/1864	8/15/1872
Noonan, Jermiah	1814	12/2/1901
Noonan, Julia	1836	12/28/1886
Norton, Elizabeth	NBDR	NDDR
Norton, Mary w/o James Norton.	1803	5/22/1877
Nosamanna, Bertha (nee Sztracks)	7/7/1891	?/7/1914
Novorolsky, John	1877	1909
Nowotarski, Betty M. (nee Mittower)	1932	NDDR
Nowotarski, Florence w/o Frank J. Nowotarski.	1905	1943
Nowotarski, Francis C. Seaman 4th Cl. U.S. Navy W.W. II.	1926	1980
Nowotarski, Frank J. h/o Florence Nowotarski.	1894	1973
Nowotarski, Richard H.	1932	NDDR
Nowotarski, Walter J.	1886	1923

- O -

Name	NBDR	NDDR
Oblinger, Amelia L.	1843	1925
Oblinger, Benjamin T.	1843	1914
Oblinger, Elmer Raymond	6/25/1871	10/15/1875
Oblinger, Julia H. (nee Maloney) w/o B. F. Oblinger.	8/12/1847	12/27/1873
Obold, George C.	NBDR	NDDR
Obold, Josephine M.	NBDR	NDDR
O'Brien, Ellen Raised St. Catharine's Orphan Asylum.	July 1874	Dec. 1893
Ochocki, Mary (nee Jankowski)	6/8/1884	9/1/1970
Ochocki. Stanley	5/8/1880	10/24/1960
O'Connor, Patrick Born, in Ireland. h/o Margaret O'Connor.	3/7/1820	2/8/1891
O'Donnell, ? d/o Williamm J. & Alice M. O'Donnell.	12/6/1929	1/7/1937
O'Donnell, Alice M. w/o William J. O'Donnell.	6/24/1864	4/3/1930
O'Donnell, Margaret	1818	4/10/1892
O'Donnell, William J. h/o Alice M. O'Donnell.	7/12/1867	12/19/1957

O'Grattis, Anna	6/7/1904	5/5/1929
O'Grattis, Mary	1884	1929
O'Hara, John	1826	7/14/1891
Born, Cavan County, Ireland. h/o Julia O'Hara.		
O'Hara, Julia	NBDR	8/5/1900
w/o John O'Hara.		
Ohlinger, ?	1873	1946
Ohlinger, William	1894	1973
Olvieri, Michiele	1898	1918
O'Malley, Mary Ann	1785	12/1/1868
O'Meara, Timothy	1864	1934
O'Neil, ?	1832	1860
w/o Bartholomew O'Neil.		
O'Neil, Bartholomew	1827	1862
h/o ? O'Neil.		
O'Neil, Mary	NBDR	NDDR
Infant d/o Bartholomew O'Neil & ?		
O'Neil, John	4/27/1839	1/7/1902
h/o Margaret C. O'Neil.		
O'Neil, Margaret C.	NBDR	9/3/1904
w/o John O'Neil.		
O'Neill, Annie	3/10/1822	6/6/1888
w/o Daniel O'Neill.		
O'Neill, Annie Maria	NBDR	NDDR
O'Neill, Daniel	1817	8/29/1894
h/o Annie O'Neill.		
O'Neill, Edward	7/18/1826	10/22/1882
Born, County Limerick, Ireland.		
O'Neill, Elizabeth	NBDR	NDDR
O'Neill, James H.	2/23/1865	2/1/1876
Orchowski, Catherine P.	1879	1949
Orchowski, John	1876	1954
O'Reilly, Ann	1855	6/15/1857
O'Reilly, Anna E.	1882	1954
O'Reilly, Catharine C. (nee Felix)	6/17/1815	7/9/1893
O'Reilly, Elizabeth B.	4/26/1820	12/28/1885
O'Reilly, Eugene A.	1882	1956
O'Reilly, James P.	6/26/1836	10/7/1848
O'Reilly, Jerome P.	1912	1969
O'Reilly, Mary A.	3/23/1855	3/20/1890
O'Reilly, Mollie B.	8/15/1859	3/20/1902

Name	Birth	Death
O'Reilly, O.	NBDR	5/19/1902
Born, Ireland.		
O'Reilly, Patrick	3/14/1810	1/16/1881
O'Reilly, Willie	10/9/1857	11/5/1858
Orlando, Angela	1867	1915
Orlando, Anthony	11/13/1918	10/20/1930
Orlando, Bambino	1887	1914
Orlando, Frank P.	1884	1961
Orlando, Giuseppe	1881	1957
Orlando,. Jennie	1891	1912
Orlando, Maria L.	1893	1973
Orlando, Nina	1895	1972
Orlando, Vincent	1919	1921
Oros, Joseph	4/16/1905	7/8/1905
O'Rourke, Charles P.	1864	1935
O'Rourke, Joseph	12/1/1884	10/11/1885
O'Rourke, Mary M.	1856	1937
Oswald, Madelin (nee Grill)	NBDR	NDDR
Ott, Adam	9/22/1818	9/17/1865
Ott, Agnes	10/20/1856	7/14/1939
Ott, Anna M.	9/16/1817	9/16/1848
Ott, Anna Mabelle	1919	1919
Ott, Anna Marie	9/16/1839	4/2/1902
Ott, Caroline	NBDR	NDDR
Ott, Caroline	4/1/1817	4/12/1880
Ott, Dolires Theresa	1931	1931
Ott, George F.	9/3/1874	4/12/1970
Ott, Helena	1852	11/14/1852
Ott, Joseph	NBDR	NDDR
Ott, Josephine	5/1/1854	11/4/1886
Ott, Magnus	9/5/1847	2/9/1916
Ott, Magnus M.	1895	1961
Ott, Martin	4/19/1846	7/16/1881
Ott, Mary M. (nee Brady)	7/30/1852	12/4/1905
w/o John A. Ott.		
Ott, Mathias	1/15/1834	12/10/1909
Ott, Teresa C.	5/1/1854	10/24/1900
w/o Francis J. Ott.		
Otten, Albert J.	1860	1897
Otten, Joseph	10/7/1812	7/1/1908
Otten, Martha	1/28/1822	10/3/1894
Owens, Daniel	12/11/1829	8/4/1908
Member of Co K 128th Inf Regt Pa Volunteers Civil War.		

- P -

Pace, Antoinette	1887	1967
w/o Giovanni Pace.		
Pace, Giovanni	1889	1948
h/o Antoinette Pace.		
Pace, Julia	1/14/1915	9/22/1929
d/o Giovanni & Antoinette Pace.		
Pagano, Joseph	NBDR	1/11/1916
Palaferre, Salvatore	10/26/1914	1/28/1916
Palugh, Anna	1/1/1871	7/2/1916
Palugh, Joseph	3/8/1864	1/10/1924
Pantaleo, Alberico	1884	1932
Pantaleo, Frances J.	1914	1934
Papan, Kaytan	1889	1968
Parents, Raffaele	4/20/1870	8/26/1911
Parker, Mary T.	7/30/1884	7/19/1968
Paul, Ann	1825	March 1869
w/o Urban Paul.		
Paul, Urban	1804	1/7/1869
h/o Ann Paul.		
Paulus, Adam C.	6/15/1835	1/22/1901
Paulus, Annie M.	6/9/1836	11/9/1882
Paulus, Joseph	1/26/1840	11/9/1901
Paulus, Theresia	7/20/1845	10/1/1894
Pauza, A. H.	1926	1981
Pavik, Anna	1885	1936
Pavik, Helen	1912	1967
Paavlik, Anna	NBDR	1907
Pearson, Edward P.	1818	March 1889
h/o Frederica (nee Smith) Pearson.		
Pearson, Frederica (nee Smith)	11/1/1810	8/31/1885
w/o Edward P. Pearson.		
Pearson, Mary	NBDR	NDDR
Pellegrino, Dinino, Jr.	1918	1921
Pelliccioltti, Aurora	9/27/1879	5/16/1916
Pepe, Anna	1873	1947

Name	Birth	Death
Pepe, Charles E. T/3 Fiscal Office, U.S. Army W.W. II.	1909	1965
Pepe, Donato h/o Maria Pepe.	1860	1942
Pepe, F. G.	NBDR	NDDR
Pepe, Francesca E. (nee Pietro)	NBDR	NDDR
Pepe, Frank	1908	1910
Pepe, Frank g.	1868	1943
Pepe, Giovanna	1844	1914
Pepe, Joseph	1887	1907
Pepe, Maria w/o Donato Pepe.	1862	1905
Pepe, Mary A.	1904	NDDR
Pepe, Peter	1863	1932
Pepe, Raffaele	1/16/1823	9/28/1908
Pepe, Rose	1884	1958
Pepe, Thomas P.	1899	NDDR
Powalski, Jozef	1874	1891
Powell, Elizabeth d/o John & Barbara Powell.	NBDR	NDDR
Prestat, Eloise	11/1/1817	1/5/1897
Pribula, Mary E.	9/2/1895	3/3/1915
Przepiurg, Annie C.	3/18/1867	6/19/1947
Przepiurg, Anthony	1/1/1865	8/18/1941
Przybylski, Joseph	1866	1959
Pucciarelli, Mary Ellen	1870	1959
Pucciarelli, Seerafino	1857	1942
Puccini, Ammunziatga	1856	1909
Puccini, Salvatore	1854	1913
Puccini, Ulysess G.	1875	1937
Puwelle, Arnold	1/14/1809	9/15/1879
Puwelle, Margaret (nee Ritner)	1/5/1821	12/4/1889

- Q -

Name	Birth	Death
Quaglia, Antonio	1883	6/4/1910
Quaglia, Giulio	5/8/1889	11/12/1913
Quigiage,. Bodanza G.	2/1/1885	10/7/1915
Quinlan, Mary w/o Patrick Quinlan.	1811	1892
Quinlan, Patrick h/o Mary Quinlan.	1813	1889

Name	Birth	Death
Quinn, Michael C.	10/29/1861	11/28/1947
h/o Rose A. Quinn.		
Quinn, Rose A.	4/1/1863	3/2/1916
w/o Michael C. Quinn.		
Quinn, Rosa T.	9/19/1854	4/19/1900
Buried in Howdin plot.		

- R -

Name	Birth	Death
Raab, Jon	12/12/1888	2/1/1890
s/o George & Genevieve Raab.		
Raduazzo, A. Maria	1885	5/5/1909
Raduazzo, ?	2/23/1897	6/13/1897
Raimondi, Annunciata S.	1879	1952
Rainmondi, Giuseppi M.	1878	1938
Ramsey, Antoinette	1914	1946
Ramsey, Catharine	1/30/1917	3/24/1929
Randazzo, Diego	1892	1914
Rank, Elizabeth	4/9/1809	6/20/1889
Rank, Rosa E.	11/22/1857	11/22/1891
d/o P. D. Rank.		
Rapino, Luicci	NBDR	NDDR
Rasmussen, Cecelika	1882	1893
Rasmussen, Charles	1887	1893
Rasmussen, John	1828	1895
Rasmussen, Mary	1858	1912
Rasmussen, Raymond	1884	1885
Rasumussen, Carl	1855	1894
Ratajczak, Agnieszka	1/8/1860	10/12/1925
w/o Antoni Ratajczak.		
Ratajczak, Antoni	4/24/1862	10/27/1940
h/o Agnieszka Ratajczak.		
Ratajczak, Clarence t.	1911	1943
Sgt Co D 397th Inf 100th Div W.W. II; KIA		
Ratajczak, John A.,	6/9/1891	10/18/1949
Pvt 56th Engineers Pa W.W. I		
Ratajczak, Mary M.	1882	1948
w/o Thomas J. Ratajczak.		
Ratajczak, Thomas J.	1878	1940
Rathman, Charles	NBDR	NDDR
Rathman, Jacob	1840	1918
Rathman, Susan	1848	1917

Raul, Christian	3/10/1810	2/6/1894
Raul, Elizabeth	2/10/1812	12/16/1890
Ravel, Catharine E.	1864	1913
Ravel, Elizabeth	12/9/1840	4/6/1913
Ravel, George	9/17/1833	9/12/1910
Ray, John	3/17/1830	2/24/1898
Reads, John	3/12/1834	12/9/1856

        s/o James & Margaret Reads.

Ready, Mary	NBDR	NDDR

        w/o Michael rfeady.

Ready, Rose A.	1819	5/30/1881
Ream, Urban	NBDR	NDDR
Rebzinska, Anna E.	1890	1899
Rebzinska, Anthony	1846	1918
Rebzinska, Frances	1856	19??
Rebzinska, George A.	1892	1923
Rebzinska, Harry A.	1888	1892
Reddy, Eddie C.	5/10/1886	5/15/1888

        s/o Alfred J. & Kate Reddy.

Reedy, Bridget A.	NBDR	7/13/1943
Reedy, Mary	NBDR	11/20/1890
Reedy, Mary A.	NBDR	4/25/1922
Reedy, Michael A.	NBDR	2/19/1902
Reedy, Patrick	NBDR	1/13/1897
Regenfuse, Catharine	2/10/1812	3/5/1874
Regenfuse, Elizabeth	NBDR	NDDR
Regenfuse, Harry I.	NBDR	NDDR
Regenfuse, Henry K.	NBDR	NDDR

        Corp Co I 179th Inf Regt Pa Volunteers Civil War.

Regenfuse, John	1/1/1800	10/28/1866
Regenfuse, Rebecca	NBDR	NDDR
Rehr, Amelia (nee Wast?)	7/5/1862	1882

        w/o Howard D. Rehr.

Rehr, Caroline	1832	1891
Rehr, Catharine (nee Orth)	10/26/1832	5/18/1917

        w/o John W. Rehr.

Rehr, Franklin W.	1860	1861
Rehr, Howard D.	12/18/1858	10/8/1885

        h/o Amelia (nee Wast?) Rehr. s/o John W. & Catharine (nee Orth) Rehr.

Rehr, John W.	10/5/1830	4/27/1896

        h/o Catharine (nee Orth) Rehr.

Rehr, Ralph R.	1908	1910
Rehr, Richard	1869	1877

Name	Birth	Death
Rehr, William	1827	1877
Rehr, Willikam	1863	1864
Rehr, William J. A.	2/2/1882	10/3/1897
Rehrenbach, Susanna w/o Carl Rehrenbach.	1820	1885
Rehrer, Warren	1/11/1882	10/8/1918
Reicheneder, Anna Maria	9/5/1826	11/9/1869
Reicheneder, Barbara	11/12/18??	2/29/187?
Reicheneder, Bernard s/o Irvin & Emily Reicheneder.	6/12/1915	11/14/1915
Reicheneder, George h/o Mary A. Reicheneder.	9/3/1855	3/15/1909
Reicheneder, John	12/17/1856	11/1/1939
Reicheneder, John J. s/o George & Mary A. Reicheneder.	7/6/1880	11/14/1893
Reicheneder, Kate	1/28/1859	9/3/1918
Reicheneder, Mary A. w/o George Reicheneder.	8/25/1855	1/23/1926
Reicheneder, Michael Born, Salern.	4/19/1825	2/13/1899
Reicher, John A.	NBDR	NDDR
Reichert, John	1/14/1813	3/19/1883
Reichert, Rebecca	4/13/1818	3/20/1894
Reiley, Annie w/o John Reiley.	1824	9/11/1904
Reiley, John	NBDR	5/28/1909
Reiley, John h/o Annie Reiley.	1822	2/22/1894
Reilly, Catharine	1836	10/1/1875
Reilly, Ellen Elizabeth (Nun) Taken vows as Sister Veronica.	8/22/1850	12/12/1876
Reilly, Joseph J.	10/12/1910	6/17/1969
Reilly, Mary Johanna	3/10/1795	4/10/1877
Reilly, Patrick	1836	3/2/1892
Reilly, Richard	1844	5/21/1872
Reilly, Richard Born, Ireland.	3/8/1798	1/9/1872
Reilly, Robert	7/12/1854	11/27/1872
Reilly, Thomas John died at age of 70 years.	NBDR	NDDR
Reinbold,. Caroline	1858	1927
Reinbold, Magdalena	1824	1896
Reinbold, Simon	1828	1907

Reiner, Anna   1860   1867
Reiner, Anna Augusta   8/26/1868   2/4/1890
     d/o John B. & Catharine Reiner.
Reiner, Elizabeth   1858   1867
Reiner, John B.   1824   1872
     h/o Catharine Reiner.
Reiner, John Henry   11/22/1858   1/1/1884
     s/o John B. & Catharine Reiner.
Reiner, Katharine   1863   1867

Reiner, Mary Catharine   3/13/1840   11/13/1897
Reiner, William Jacob   3/1/1832   10/11/1867

Reinert, Agnes W.   1898   1941

Reisinger, George W.   7/17/1846   7/23/1890
Reisinger, Josephine   11/1/1845   12/15/1922
Reisinger, Mary   2/10/1827   8/10/1895
Reisinger, Wolfgang   10/20/1820   12/31/1897

Reismann, Christian   2/24/1820   12/21/1884
Reismann, Elizabeth   2/?/1821   3/17/1893

Reitnauer, Sarah A.   1866   1949

Remp, Anna Maria   4/15/1831   6/27/1853
     Born, Darnstadt, Germany. Lived U. S. 3 weeks.

Repplier, Catharine   1781   4/20/1870
     w/o John George Repplier.
Repplier,, John George   1/1/1766   1/18/1837
     h/o Catharine Reppl;ier. Born, Strasburg, France.
Repplier, Louisa A.   1799   10/12/1886

Resch, Jacob M.   1860   1930
     h/o Julia A. Resch.
Resch, Julia A.   1865   1931
     w/o Jacob M. Resch.
Resch, Lille   1864   1922
Resch, Louisa   NBDR   11/13/1905

Ressler, Leona M.   1870   1872

Reuth, John J.   2/26/1884   7/10/1910
     Member Co D 29th Regt Spanish American War.
     s/o Martin & Mary Reuth.
Reuth, Martin   2/25/1845   2/11/1923
     h/o Mary Reuth.
Reuth, Mary   4/8/1851   1/16/1923
     w/o Martin Reuth.

Reuthner, Adolph   12/3/1847   1/13/1854

Name	Birth	Death
Rheinwalt, William G.	1879	1919
Rheinwalt, Joseph	12/13/1806	12/12/1881
Born, Rheinfalz, Bavaria, Germany.		
Rice, Christopher C.	4/4/1845	8/21/1873
Richards, Augustus G.	2/17/1846	1/10/1884
Richards, Blanche D. (nee Cox)	1888	1975
w/o Samuel L. Richards.		
Richards, Charles A.	1857	1919
Richards, Charles J.	1921	1973
Sgt. U.S. Air Force W.W. II.		
s/o Samuel L. & Blanche D. (nee Cox) Richards.		
Richards, J. Aaron	1882	1917
Richards, Samuel L.	1890	1961
h/o Blanche D. (nee Cox) Richards.		
Cpl. Hdqts Co. 26th Inf. W.W. I.		
Richards, Thomas,	NBDR	NDDR
Richman, Johanna	1802	1884
Rick, George Daniel	1853	12/5/1854
s/o George Rick & Maria Anna Deppen.		
Rickert, Anna M.	12/25/1847	4/14/1908
Rickert, Charles	9/29/1872	11/16/1947
Rickert, Joseph A.	3/23/1838	7/18/1898
Rieger, Anthony	6/12/1828	1/21/1906
Rieger, Frank	1871	1924
Rieger, Katharine	2/23/1830	1/11/1905
Rieger, Leopold	1856	1931
Rieger, Mary	1860	1927
Riesle, Maria Agatha	2/9/1849	9/9/1870
Rill, Amanda	1853	1902
Rill, Augustus	1836	1925
Rill, Augustus J.	1888	1975
Rippel, Henry	NBDR	NDDR
Rippel, Mary	NBDR	NDDR
Ritner, Carolina	1852	3/17/1852
d/o Joseph Ritner & Lydia Ekuguent.		
Ritner, Catharine	4/17/1803	4/13/1858
Ritner, Frances	1/5/1821	3/3/1843
Ritner, George	NBDR	NDDR
Ritner, George E.	12/9/1889	NDDR
h/o Nellie F. Ritner.		
Ritner, George L.	3/5/1846	5/19/1913
Member Co I 195th Inf Pa Volunteers Civil War.		

Ritner, Jacob	6/6/1792	6/26/1854
Ritner, Joseph F.	4/26/1869	3/29/1912
Member Co D 6th Regt Pa Volunteers S.A. War.		
Ritner, Leah A.	1/31/1886	4/18/1887
Ritner, Mary K.	8/14/1855	6/7/1941
Ritner, Nellie F.	6/9/1886	1/3/1921
w/o George E. Ritner.		
Ritner, Sarah C.	2/11/1827	4/12/1878
Rohrbach, Albert E.	11/19/1861	2/11/1894
Rohrbach, David	5/24/1847	1/3/1924
Rohrbach, John D.	1882	1925
Rohrbach, Joseph	9/?/1829	3/?/1906
h/o Sarah Rohrbach.		
Rohrbach, Sarah	1/3/1832	7/15/1885
w/o Joseph Rohrbach.		
Rohrbach, Sarah	3/26/1843	12/10/1920
Rojer, John Krize	1868	5/3/1915
Rolinski, ?	NBDR	NDDR
Infant son of John & Estelle Rolinski.		
Romanstraka, Rodzeni	5/11/1908	5/17/1908
Rosalia, Galata	12/27/1856	3/28/1930
Rossi, Antonio	1862	5/29/1915
Roth, Andrew	9/8/1834	5/17/1906
h/o Pauline B. Roth.		
Roth, M. Clara	3/20/1869	9/5/1888
d/o Andrew & Pauline B. Roth.		
Roth, Pauline B.	7/4/1841	4/5/1920
Rothant, Elisabeth Maria	1851	3/10/1853
d/o Joseph Rothant & Frances Kurtz.		
Rothaupt, Benerdina	1818	1895
w/o John Augustus Rothaupt.		
Rothaupt, John Augustus	1815	11/4/1887
h/o Benerdina Rothaupt.		
Rothaupt, John Augustus	1876	6/18/1904
Rothenberger, Charles	12/23/1824	12/19/1887
Rothenberger, Magdalena	6/27/1828	11/1/1887
Rothharpt, Joseph	3/16/1812	6/8/1882
Rotting, Antonia	1884	1929
Rotting, Antonio	1889	1931

Name	Born	Died
Rourke, Bridget	1858	1919
Rourke, Bridget	1829	1/3/1903
w/o Owen Rourke.		
Rourke, James J.	12/9/1859	12/23/1923
Rourke, John	8/12/1831	NDDR
Rourke, Michael J.	4/8/1869	8/28/1896
Rourke, Owen	1825	2/12/1870
h/o Bridget Rourke.		
Rourke, S. Ann	8/3/1862	6/26/1887
Rowe, Juin W.	NBDR	NDDR
Rucski, ?	NBDR	NDDR
Rudden, Bernard	1838	8/2/1899
h/o mary Rudden.		
Rudden, Mary	1830	7/15/1891
w/o Bernard Rudden.		
Rudden, Sarah	1860	6/17/1907
Ruesch, Mary M.	1825	1894
Ruesch, Peter	1821	1879
Rufe, Charles	7/9/1848	2/8/1931
h/o Emma R. Rufe.		
Rufe, Emma R.	2/28/1853	11/14/1907
w/o Charles Rufe.		
Rufe, Lewis W.	10/20/1872	12/6/1892
s/o Charles & Emma R. Rufe.		
Ruhefant?, ?	NBDR	NDDR
Russo, Domenico	4/25/1873	11/30/1918
Russo, Febronia	12/26/1924	2/26/1928
Russo, Rose	8/26/1910	7/26/1926
Rutz, Apollonia	7/17/1817	11/?/1877
w/o John Rutz.		
Rutz, John	12/18/1811	7/20/1852
h/o Apollonia Rutz. Born, Heseberg, County of Waldfisch, Germany.		
Ryan, Anna M.	1879	10/14/1937
w/o William P. Ryan.		
Ryan, Francis P.	6/9/1856	9/26/1885
Ryan, Hannah M.	5/3/1819	1/24/1892
Ryan, Joanna	11/27/1858	1/2/1896
Ryan, John	6/24/1812	2/17/1866
Ryan, Rev. Peter J.	1854	1920
Ryan, Rosanna C.	11/4/1849	9/26/1892
Ryan, Susan D.	7/26/1861	10/2/1887
Ryan, Thomas A.	1889	1941
Ryan, William P.	6/13/1856	3/13/1935
h/o Anna M. Ryan.		

- S -

Name		
Sacco, Geovanna Maria	1880	1949
Sacco, Maria	1910	1918
Sacco, Thomas	1918	1955
Sacco, Vito antonio	1877	1827
Sadlowski, Mary A.	1888	1954
w/o Valentine Sadlowski.		
Sadlowski, Valentine	1875	1950
h/o Mary A. Sadlowski.		
St. Clair, Bridget	8/17/1849	4/7/1880
w/o Daniel St. Clair.		
St. Clair, Catharine (nee Ritner)	11/11/1818	4/15/1880
St. Clair, Daniel	1845	1933
h/o Bridget St. Clair.		
St. Clair, Samuel	2/2/????	2/8/1886
St. Clair, Samuel C.	10/8/1875	9/7/1899
Sakiewicz, Francis J.	1908	1961
Photographer 1st Class U.S. Navy W.W. II.		
Sakiewicz, Jan	1866	1946
Sakiewicz, Mary Ann	NBDR	NDDR
Sakiewicz, Maryanna	1865	1946
Salino, Antonino	1863	1906
Salino, Sebastiana	1861	1936
Saloka, John S.	1910	1975
Salona, Mus Jan?	5/16/1879	10/11/1916
Salvatore, Giuseppe	1/7/1915	6/10/1922
Samolis, Katharine	1863	6/5/1911
Samsel, Frank	10/6/1905	11/13/1906
Samsel, Frank	5/28/1909	8/26/1909
Santangelo, Austin	1912	1916
Santangelo, Giuseppe	1881	1916
Santospereto, Maria	3/7/1901	1925
w/o Sebastiano Ninfo.		
Saquelli, Antonio	8/9/1915	10/5/1916
s/o Joseph & Rose Saquelli.		
Sad, Walentin	2/14/1896	4/5/1912
Sattler, George J.	4/24/1860	9/3/1925

Sattler, Kate	2/4/1865	12/17/1898
Sattler, Rosa	NBDR	NDDR
Sauer, Anna Ora	2/22/1810	1/10/1855
w/o Johannas Sauer.		
Sauer, Apollania	9/14/1838	3/8/1912
Sauer, Augustus	NBDR	NDDR
Sauer, Catharine	NBDR	NDDR
Sauer, Cecilia	NBDR	NDDR
Sauer, Christopher	12/25/1827	11/7/1893
h/o Eva A. Sauer.		
Sauer, Clara	NBDR	NDDR
Sauer, Elizabeth M.	1869	1910
Sauer, Eva A.	1831	8/29/1912
w/o Christopher Sauer.		
Sauer, Johannas	6/12/1808	12/5/1892
h/o Anna Ora Sauer.		
Sauer, John	1844	1908
h/o Margaret Sauer.		
Sauer, Paul	NBDR	NDDR
Sauer, Philip	1845	5/5/1906
Sauer, William	NBDR	NDDR
Sauter, Amelia	1873	1944
Sauter, Amelia E.	7/17/1893	12/2/1901
Sauter, Andrew	3/5/1838	10/17/1906
h/o Elizabeth Sauter.		
Sauter, Elizabeth	10/10/1837	11/8/1922
w/o Andrew Sauter.		
Sauter, Richard W.	1870	1941
h/o Rosie M. Sauter.		
Sauter, Rosie M.	6/12/1873	2/12/1896
w/o Richard W. Sauter.		
Saylor, Elizabeth E.	1865	1929
w/o Henry Saylor.		
Saylor, Irvin H.	1893	1908
s/o Henry & Elizabeth E. Saylor.		
Scaramella, Dortea	7/28/1848	4/21/1924
Scaramella, Salvatore	3/31/1844	11/27/1907
Scarffe, Angelina	1897	1935
Scarffe, Ralph	1924	1925
Scarffe, Ralph A.	1926	1928
Schaefer, Catharine	2/1/186?	?/28/187?
d/o J. George & Fredericka (nee Vogel) Schaefer.		
Schaefer, Catharine T.	2/5/1858	4/1/1922
w/o John Schaefer.		
Schaefer, Charles f.	1865	1956
Schaefer, Fredericka (nee Vogel)	7/17/1834	1/16/1910
w/o J. George Schaefer.		

Schaefer, George A.	8/12/1870	1/9/1889
s/o J. George & Fredericka (nee Vogel) Schaefer.		
Schaefer, J. George	2/19/1826	12/3/1889
h/o Fredericka (nee Vogel) Schaefer.		
Schaefer, John J.	1864	1928
Schaefer, Mary A.	1859	1938
Schaefer, Theresia	10/10/1860	6/23/1867
d/o J. George & Fredericka (nee Vogel) Schaefer.		
Schaeffer, Alice S. (nee Seaman)	1870	1904
Scheck, Andrew	8/15/1824	12/4/1888
Scheck, Gertrude E.	9/9/1886	11/24/1890
d/o P. & Elizabeth Scheck.		
Scheck, Mary	3/23/1832	8/26/1924
Scheck, Mary C.	9/24/1884	11/10/1887
d/o P. & Elizabeth Scheck.		
Scheck, Mary V.	3/9/1889	4/13/1903
d/o P. & Elizabeth Scheck.		
Schell, Annie M.	3/31/1871	5/15/1887
d/o Michael & Magdalena A. Schell.		
Schell, Magdalena A.	4/17/1844	1/20/1912
w/o Michael Schell.		
Schell, Michael	10/17/1841	12/16/1924
h/o Magdalena A. Schell.		
Schera, Anastasia	1855	1917
Schlegel, Christo;pher J.	1893	1951
Pvt Inf unassigned W.W. I.		
Schlegel, Henry J.	6/25/1856	10/18/1937
h/o Mary T. Schlegel.		
Schlegel, Mary T.	11/17/1866	11/2/1922
w/o Henry J. Schlegel.		
Schlevinski, Eva	NBDR	1905
Schlevinski, Frank	NBDR	1954
Schlevinski, Joseph	NBDR	1935
Schlotterbeck, Josephine	NBDR	1913
Schmidt, Anna C.	1855	1924
Schmidt, Barbara	1879	1918
Schmidt, Margaret	1834	1923
w/o Sebastian Schmidt.		
Schmidt, Sebastian	1824	1903
h/o Margaret Schmidt.		
Schmieder. Cecellia	1884	1897
d/o Lewis & Emma Schmieder.		
Schmieder, Emma	1861	1953
w/o Lewis Schmieder.		

Name	NBDR	NDDR
Schmieder, Helen	1894	1970
d/o Lewis & Emma Schmieder.		
Schmieder, Henry J.	1856	1913
Schmieder, Lewis	1861	1894
h/o Emma Schmieder.		
Schmieder, Mary A.	1854	1908
Schmitt, Children not named	NBDR	NDDR
Children of Geroge J. & Ellen B. Schmitt.		
Schmitt, Barbara	12/10/1819	8/27/1899
Schmitt, Catharine E.	2/5/1872	11/1/1894
Schmitt, Clara	8/12/1827	2/6/1919
Schmitt, Ellen B.	1/7/1863	8/4/1914
w/o George J. Schmitt.		
Schmitt, Frank	1853	1916
Schmitt, Franz B.	3/11/1827	2/14/1896
Schmitt, Geroge J.	8/30/1855	6/9/1912
h/o Ellen B. Schmitt.		
Schmitt, Jacob Henry	1852	6/23/1854
s/o John Schmitt & Isabell Leiney.		
Schmitt, John	5/15/1814	7/12/1874
h/o Isabella Leiney.		
Schmitt, John B.	1/29/1874	9/6/1892
Schmitt, John J.	9/16/1836	10/24/1918
h/o Nathalia Schmitt.		
Schmitt, Joseph R.	2/3/1879	11/13/1898
Schmitt, Lawrence	1/5/1829	10/25/1913
Schmitt, Lawrence W.	1857	1911
Schmitt, Mary Ann	11/10/1869	7/23/1881
Schmitt, Nathalia	1/12/1837	5/27/1924
w/o John J. Schmitt.		
Schmittinger, John	9/7/1816	8/2/1889
Schmittinger, John C.	7/21/1891	7/10/1898
Schnabel, Infant	NBDR	1898
Schnabel, Adam R.	1874	1875
s/o John & Barbra (nee Ruffner) Schnabel.		
Schnabel, Alexander R.	1873	1873
s/o John & Barbara (nee Ruffner) Schnabel.		
Schnabel, Barbara (nee Ruffner)	1836	1909
w/o John Schnabel.		
Schnabel, Charles R.	1859	1879
s/o John & Barbara (nee Ruffner) Schnabel.		
Schnabel, John	5/15/1794	1/9/1860
h/o Susanna Schnabel.		
Schnabel, John	1833	1884
h/o Barbara (nee Ruffner) Schanbel.		
s/o John & Susanna Schnabel.		
Schnabel, Matilda R.	1864	1882
d/o John & Barbara (nee Ruffner) Schanbel.		
Schanbel, Nicholas R.	1868	1882
s/o John & Barbara (nee Ruffner) Schnabel.		

Name	Birth	Death
Schnabel, Susanna w/o John Schnabel.	3/20/1794	8/3/1875
Schnable, Ellen w/o Henry R. Schnable.	12/21/1861	4/16/1898
Schnable, Henry R. h/o Ellen Schnable.	1855	1947
Schneider, Andreas	6/11/1865	3/18/1892
Schneider, Andreas G.	1/5/1824	11/9/1875
Schneider, Elizabeth	8/20/1834	8/30/1915
Schneider, Mary A.	6/17/1871	5/31/1915
Schnepf, Joseph h/o Margaretta Schnepf.	1816	6/17/1877
Schnepf, Margaretta w/o Joseph Schnepf.	1821	4/9/1902
Schoeninger, John	5/12/1812	11/27/1879
Schoeninger, Anna Catharina	4/13/1873	11/11/1875
Schott, Esther V. d/o Augustus & Sarah Schott.	1/28/1887	9/19/1889
Schott, Sarah w/o Augustus Schott.	6/9/1849	11/6/1910
Schroeder, Anna (nee Leisz0	NBDR	1/22/1929
Schultz, Joseph B.	8/19/1885	10/17/1918
Schwalb, Albert s/o George & Mary E. Schwalb.	12/?/1860	5/11/1875
Schwalb, George h/o Mary E. Schwalb.	6/22/1810	12/21/1889
Schwalb, Mary E. w/o Geroge Schwalb.	3/25/1817	1/4/1892
Schwander, Frederick J.	2/2/1885	8/2/1915
Schwank, Catharine E.	5/27/1819	4/17/1900
Schwank, Ellen w/o Adam Schwank.	1834	1887
Schwank, George A.	1852	1912
Schwank, John	1/6/1817	9/25/1895
Schwank, John	6/2/1860	11/6/1896
Schwank, Joseph Francis s/o Adam Schwank & Maria Elisabeth Hartmann.	1851	3/8/1852
Schwank, Maria Eleanore d/o Adam & Maria Hartmann.	7/25/1849	11/3/1853
Schwank, Rose	2/28/1868	11/2/1892
Schwartz, Arthur	1905	1944
Schwartz, Catherine	9/26/1861	6/12/1927

Schwartz, Franklin	NBDR	5/27/1894
s/o Franklin C. & Mary E. (nee Crimmens) Schwartz.		
Schwartz, Franklin C.	1862	1922
h/o Mary E. (nee Crimmens) Schwartz.		
Schwartz, Leo F.	1895	1964
Schwartz, Mary E. (nee Crimmens)	1863	1947
w/o Franklin C. Schwartz.		
Schwartz, Sylvester	NBDR	1/1/1899
s/o Franklin C. & Mary E. (nee Crimmens) Schwartz.		
Schweitzer, ?	12/2/1892	9/28/1944
Schweitzer, Elizabeth G.	1855	NDDR
Schweitzer, Joseph J.	1852	1905
Schwemmer, Casper	1847	1908
Schwemmer, Ernst S.	1876	1947
Was in Armed Forces Spanish American War.		
Schwemmer, Jacob	1889	1892
Schwemmer, Mary	1845	1926
Schwemmer, Oswcar	1874	1902
Schwoerer, Katie	1865	1882
d/o L. & E. Schwoerer.		
Schwoerer, Leopold	1838	1903
Screpesi, Paolina	7/29/1909	3/21/1916
Seery, Lillian R.	1884	1951
Seifert, Catharine	2/15/1829	1903
w/o Joseph Seifert.		
Seifert, Sarah (nee Kissling)	2/2/1812	7/11/1879
w/o William Seifert.		
Seifert, William	10/29/1799	10/20/1867
h/o Sarah (nee Kissling) Seifert.		
Seiling, ?	12/24/1832	6/29/1922
Member of Co B 167th Regt Pa Volunteers Civil War.		
Seiling, Sarahg A.	6/9/1842	2/27/1899
Seisler, Anna M.	9/3/1902	5/8/1904
Sekulski, Florence Marie	4/12/1888	5/7/1969
Sekulski, John Joseph	11/1/1877	12/30/1942
Sellinger, Joseph	NBDR	NDDR
Serafino, Paul E., Jr.	1951	1972
Serba, Mary Ann	8/18/1867	12/2/1909

Name	Birth	Death
Sewicki, Raymond A.	1893	1959
Seyfert, Anna M.	NBDR	NDDR
w/o Daniel Seyfert.		
Seyfeert, Daniel	2/29/1751	5/17/1813
h/o Anna M. Seyfert.		
Seyfert, Joseph	Dec. 1752	Feb. 1821
Shade, Anna	NBDR	NDDR
Shade, Anthony	NBDR	NDDR
Shade, Arthur E., Sr.	1880	1939
Pvt Co C 1st Regt Spanish American War.		
Shade, Elizabeth	NBDR	NDDR
Shade, Eva	NBDR	NDDR
Shade, George E.	1873	1911
Corp U.S. Marine Corps.		
Shade, John	NBDR	NDDR
Shade, Mary C.	1848	1933
w/o Michael A. Shade.		
Shade, Michael A.	7/2/1844	1/10/1890
h/o Mary C. Shade. Born, Bavaria, Germany.		
Shaeffer, Anna Ludovica	1/22/1851	12/12/1851
d/o Constantine Shaeffer & Angeline Hartmann.		
Sharp, John	1818	NDDR
Sheahan, Ellen B.	1857	1936
Sheahan, Honora	1814	1899
Sheahan, Mazrtin J.	1877	1961
Sheahan, Michael	1886	1891
Sheahan, Thomas	1846	1926
Sheeran, Sister Mary Ignatia	NBDR	NDDR
Sheridan, John	1799	9/4/1865
Born, Ireland. h/o Rose Sheridan.		
Sheridan, John	1842	4/27/1863
s/o John & Rose Sheridan.		
Sheridan, Rose	1816	3/24/1866
w/o John Sheridan. Born, Ireland.		
Sherman, James	NBDR	1862
Shilling, Elizabeth C.	1863	1941
Shipper, George A.	7/18/1888	10/4/1916
Shipper, John V.	3/12/1854	5/1/1928
Shipper, Margaretha V.	3/1/1861	8/25/1915
Shiretien, Maria	4/6/1871	9/12/1891
Shusko, Joseph	1928	1930

Siegfried, Anna A.	1886	1950
w/o George A. Siegfried.		
Siegfried, George A.	1861	1946
h/o Anna A. Siegfried.		
Siegfried, William J.	1898	1974
s/o George A. & Anna A. Siegfried.		
Sieringer, Elizabeth (nee Bieringer)	1843	1891
w/o Charles Sieringer..		
Simon, Edward	NBDR	10/4/1877
h/o Rosa Simon.		
Simon, Guilhelm,	1852	Feb 1853
s//o John Simon & Sarah Rapp.		
Simon, Rosa	NBDR	NDDR
w/o Edward Simon.		
Sivak, Josef	1864	1/18/1919
Skonaszewski, Joseph	NBDR	NDDR
Skonaszewski, Sylvester S.	1893	1961
Pvt 65th Coast Artillery Corps W.W. I.		
Slavensky, George	NBDR	10/15/1921
Slavin, Catharine C.	NBDR	3/11/1968
Slavin, Charles J.	NBDR	10/6/1958
Slavin, Mary A.	NBDR	11/12/1975
Slegelmitch, John W.	4/28/1883	11/17/1918
Sloan, Michael W.	9/16/1866	6/8/1896
Smeck, Charles H.	6/18/1841	4/2/1899
Pvt Co M 2nd Regt Pa Volunteer Cavalry.		
h/o Elizabeth M. (nee St. Clair) Smeck.		
Smeck, Elizabeth M. (nee St. Clair)	12/24/1841	8/11/1906
w/o Charles H. Smeck.		
Smelewski, Simon	11/12/1840	9/18/1920
h/o Wilhelmina Smelewski.		
Smelewski, Wilhelmina	10/1/1841	1/9/1927
w/o Simon Smelewski.		
Smith, ?	1856	12/11/1857
Smith, Anna	1877	1970
Smith, Annie E.	1878	1929
Smith, Barbara (nee Ritner)	9/27/1823	1/6/1885
w/o Joseph Smith.		
Smith, C. Levi	1911	1912
Smith, Charles F.	NBDR	NDDR
Smith, Dorothy T.	1905	1910
d/o Edward & Lucy Smith.		

	NBDR	NDDR
Smith, Eddie	NBDR	NDDR
s/o Edmond L. & Lina Smith.		
Smith, Edmond L	10/28/1829	9/11/1891
h/o Line Smith.		
Smith, Edward J.	1882	1934
h/o Lucy Smith.		
Smith, George L.	3/10/1802	9/29/1878
Smith, G. Harry	9/19/1864	6/7/1914
Smith, James A.	1903	1904
Smith, John A.	11/17/1861	2/12/1902
Smith, John H.	June 1828	4/22/1893
Born, Maython Brook County, Ireland.		
Smith, Joseph F.	1906	1943
Pvt Bn E 172nd FA W.W. II.		
Smith, Joseph T.	12/21/1825	8/6/1891
Smith, Kate	1842	1923
Smith, Lina	7/20/1835	2/28/1911
w/o Edmond L. Smith.		
Smith, Margaret R.	10/12/1801	12/31/1885
Smith, Mary	March 1829	2/3/1900
Born, Galway County, Ireland.		
Smith, Sarah A.C.	NBDR	NDDR
Smith, Susan (nee Boylan)	1853	1900
Smith, William A.	11/8/1867	1/28/1897
Smorey, Maria S.	1868	1918
Smorey, Regina	10/23/1903	11/1/1914
Smorey, Otec Andro	1862	1917
Smorey, Veronica	NBDR	11/10/1931
Snyder, ?	NBDR	NDDR
Snyder, Anna V.	1907	NDDR
Snyder, Daniel P.	1902	NDDR
Snyder, David E.	5/6/1837	3/11/1900
Pvt Co E 46th Regt Civil War.		
Snyder, Earl, Jr.	1926	1927
Snyder, Ella C.	1889	1968
Snyder, Mary Aged 10 years.	1886	9/18/1896
St. Catharine's Orphanage.		
Snyder, Marie	1906	1929
Snyder, Minnie E.	3/8/1898	5/20/1934
Sobczinski, John A.	1867	1944
Sobczinski, Magdalena	1874	1927
Sobczinski, Maryanna	12/8/1879	8/23/1910
Sokolowswki, Rose	1884	1955
Solean, Sister Mary Rose	NBDR	7/17/1861
Soloka, Mary E.	1878	1958

Souders, James A.	1856	1908
h/o Mary E. Sounders.		
Souders, James F.	1890	1970
Co M Machine Gun Co 26th Inf Regt W.W. I.		
Souders, Loraine M.	1891	1904
d/o James A. & Mary E. Souders.		
Souders, Marie G.	1894	NDDR
w/o Gerhard Souders.		
Souders, Mary E.	1875	1924
w/o James A. Souders.		
Souders, Warren J.	1902	1964
s/o James A. & Mary E. Souders.		
Sova, Jozef	1899	2/26/1918
Served in U.S. Navy.		
Sova, Matka Maria	1872	8/29/1914
Sova, Michael J.	1867	1942
Spadafora, Antonio	5/9/190?	9/9/190?
s/o Samuel Spadafora.		
Spadafora, Antonio	10/31/1868	12/11/1902
Spuhler, Catharine	6/15/1819	12/7/1893
Spuhler, Catharine	5/1/1836	9/3/1873
Spuhler, Emma E.	9/4/1878	5/8/1897
Spuhler, F. X.	3/30/1814	3/5/1909
Spuhler, Francisca	10/4/1847	4/11/1926
w/o John M. Spuhler.		
Spuhler, John M.	5/15/1847	12/14/1923
h/o Francisca Spuhler.		
Spuhler, Joseph	5/7/1816	9/6/1906
Born, Switzerland.		
Spuhler, Maria Theresa	11/28/1813	5/1/1886
w/o Joseph Spuhler. Born, Schapen, Hanover, Germany.		
Spuhler, Mary Theresia	10/1/1893	11/29/1900
d/o George & Mary Spuhler.		
Spuhler, Pauline (nee Neuberger)	11/15/1847	1/16/1884
w/o George Spuhler.		
Staab, Carolina	1/17/1840	12/9/1901
Staab, Edward W.	2/2/1872	2/25/1904
Staab, Elsie	NBDR	2/15/1893
Staab, John	6/30/1833	3/31/1904
Staab, John A.	12/16/1835	3/26/1904
Staab, Josephine	6/5/1876	2/8/1902
Staab, Loretta	12/12/1889	11/14/1894
Staab, Margaret	7/12/1834	6/9/1889
Staab, Maximilian	11/10/1858	9/28/1889
Stahl, Catharine	1875	1914
Stahl, Luje D.	1897	1921
Stahl, Samuel P.	1871	1952

Name	Birth	Death
Stahl, Sarah E.	1869	1943
Stahl, William J.	1892	1903
Stanton, Catherine M.	1870	1948
Stanton, Helen J.	NBDR	1960
Stanton, James P.	1842	6/4/1908
h/o Susan S. Stanton.		
Stanton, Jane M.	NBDR	1959
Stanton, Mae (nee Kuhn)	NBDR	1948
Stanton, Michael J.	1863	1937
Stanton, Susan S.	1863	1913
w/o James P. Stanton.		
Stasek, Barbara	1881	1916
Stasek, Jozef G.	1914	1932
Stasek, Jozef S.	1873	1936
Stasek, Maria Z.	1883	1965
Steckler, Jacob A.	1845	1927
Steckler, Margaret E.	1844	1914
Stefanic, Rudolph	5/10/1908	2/5/1910
Stefanski, Andrew	1872	1951
Stefanski, Annie M.	1877	1964
Steffenberg, Amelia	6/27/1849	1/26/1879
w/o John Steffenberg.		
Steffenberg, Benjamin	4/8/1842	8/30/1880
Steffenberg, Catharine	2/2/1842	1/1/1929
w/o Joseph A. Steffenberg.		
Steffenberg, Elizabeth Genevieve	NBDR	NDDR
Steffenberg, Elizabeth C.	4/21/1849	3/17/1916
Steffenberg, Elizabeth H.	6/19/1809	12/14/1877
Steffenberg, Elizabeth H.	6/23/1869	8/7/1918
Steffenberg, Ellen A.	1/22/1871	7/22/1871
d/o Joseph & Catharine Steffenberg.		
Steffenberg, Genevieve	7/6/1831	4/7/1913
Steffenberg, John	7/17/1807	12/14/1879
Steffenberg, John	8/26/1843	12/20/1897
Steffenberg, Joseph A.	3/17/1839	9/16/1926
h/o Catharine Steffenberg.		
Stgeffenberg, Susan	5/16/1860	5/31/1927
Steffenberg, William L.	8/10/1809	2/10/1867
Stehman, George	May 1917	August 1917
Stehman, Howard W.	1892	1942
Steigerwald, John	12/27/1822	7/16/1910
h/o Sarah Steigerwald.		
Steigerwald, Lucinda	11/7/1835	9/10/1890
w/o Adam Steigerwald.		

Steigerwald, Magdalena	1861	1939
w/o Stepohen Steigerwald.		
Steigerwald, Sarah	4/17/1827	11/14/1891
w/o John Steigerwald.		
Steigerwald, Stephen	1858	1896
h/o Magdalena Steigerwald.		
Steigerwald, Stephen	1896	19??
s/o Stephen & Magdalena Steigerwald.		
Steigerwald, William A.	1892	1916
s/o Stephen & Magdalena Steigerwald.		
Was in Armed Forces W.W. I.		
Steinel, Johannes Z.	7/23/1858	10/20/1873
h/o Mariah Steinel.		
Steinel, Joseph	4/22/1853	12/10/1879
Steinel, Margaret	8/5/1827	6/26/1881
Steinel, Mariah	1852	1869
w/o Johannes Z. Steinel.		
Steinel, Peter	5/12/1819	4/22/1870
Steinel, Theobald	7/20/1856	1857
Steinle, Clara	1866	1907
Steinle, Emma	6/16/1851	4/10/1905
Steinle, Florence L.	1899	1900
Steinle, Jacob	4/26/1858	6/16/1903
Steinle, John	1859	1931
Steinle, Mary	NBDR	NDDR
Steinle, Mary	12/26/1835	1/17/1903
w/o Charles Steinle.		
Steinle, Raymond John	2/24/1892	1/24/1898
Steleton, Edward	1852	8/13/1854
s/o Edward Steleton & Maria Leyile?		
Steubner, L.H.	NBDR	NDDR
Steubner, Maggie R.	7/11/1889	11/15/1890
d/o Lewis & Mary Steubner.		
Steward, Emma A. (nee Greth)	18??	3/9/18??
w/o John A. Steward.		
Steward, Grace Helen	NBDR	NDDR
d/o John A. & Emma A. (nee Greth) Steward.		
Steward, Malcolm	NBDR	NDDR
s/o John A. & Emma A. (nee Greth) Steward.		
Stewart, A.	1/6/1822	4/23/1917
w/o Lemaul L. Stewart.		
Stewart, Donald M.	11/5/1879	4/16/1950
s/o John A. & Emma G. Stewart.		
Stewart, Elizabeth	6/17/1876	1/13/1954
d/o John A. & Emma G. Stewart.		
Stewart, Lemaul L.	9/1/1818	10/31/1853
h/o A. Stewart.		
Stewart, Wilberforce A.	1853	1891

Name	Birth	Death
Stock, Christian W.	1837	1920
Stock, Mary M.	1841	1916
Stock, Mary M.	1870	1892
Stofanik, Anna	1852	1921
Stofanik, Joseph	1846	1932
Stofko, Elezebeta m/o Helen V. Stofko.	1859	1917
Stofko, Helen V. d/o Elezebeta Stofko.	1881	1962
Stott, John H.	1870	1947
Stott, Lewis S. s/o William M. & Mary Stott.	3/21/1874	8/20/1886
Stott, Mary	NBDR	NDDR
Stott, Wellington, W.	1887	1940
Stout, George	1815	1900
Stout, Lydia	1815	1897
Stout, Rebecca A.	1848	1914
Straka, Andrew	1901	1919
Straka, Andrew M.	1911	1915
Struber, Emma A.	1902	1903
Strublar, Anna	8/15/1856	3/14/1906
Satutt, Margaret A. (nee Ready) d/o Michael & Mary Ready.	1863	10/22/1884
Sullivan, Annie	1852	11/25/1905
Sullivan, James	1843	1/26/1909
Sullivan, Lottie A.	1888	1948
Sullivan, Matthew F.	1885	1947
Sullivan, Michael J.	1884	1930
Summerfield, Joseph R.	5/11/1877	2/18/1909
Summerfield, Josephine	3/19/1852	12/11/1928
Summerfield, Martin	10/16/1840	2/15/1903
Suttake, Rozalia M.	1897	11/28/1915
Sverha, Andrej S.	5/30/1911	4/15/1914
Swank, Adam	1815	1911
Sweeney, Michael A.	1860	1909
Szmanski, John	1856	1943

Szymanski, Raymond F.	1888	1966
Szymanski, Theodora	1862	1942
Szymborski, Jozef	1855	1929
Szymborski, Maryanna	1854	1920

- T -

Tabalone, Anna	4/9/1862	4/18/1917
Tanvis, Charles V.	4/7/1862	2/26/1928
Tanvis, Emma A.	4/8/1863	10/25/1942
Tatarewicz, Anna W.	NBDR	NDDR
Thoernich, Anna	4/16/1809	1/5/1890
Thoernich, Peter	5/15/1819	10/2/1890
Thoernich, Peter H.	1854	1909
Thoernich, Wsarah A.	1865	1902
Thren, Genovefa	1/4/1826	11/23/1917
Thren, Valentin	2/17/1821	2/21/1900
Tinan, (No name)	NBDR	NDDR
s/o William P. & Mary A. Tiernan.		
Tiernan, Ann	8/15/1842	12/10/1902
w/o Bernard Tiernan.		
Tiernan, Bernard	12/24/1827	4/13/1895
h/o Ann Tiernan.		
Tiernan, Charles F.	9/20/1885	4/6/1901
Tiernan, John	12/4/1831	7/15/1898
Tiernan, Mary	12/1/1834	12/20/1904
Born, Westmeath, Ireland.		
Tiernan, Mary A.	3/17/1861	5/16/1915
w/o William P. Tiernan.		
Tiernan, Michael	1841	7/4/1858
Born, Ireland. h/o Rose Ann Tiernan.		
Tiernan, Patrick	1841	5/4/1861
Born, Westmeath, Ireland.		
Tiernan, Rose	NBDR	1/18/1845
Tiernan, Rose Ann	1802	4/8/1972
Born, Westmeath, Ireland. w/o Michael Tiernan.		
Tiernan, William P.	12/4/1861	2/11/1944
h/o Mary A. Tiernan.		
Timus, Maria	NBDR	April 1909
Timus, Joseph	1875	1942
Tischmacher, John A.	3/29/1876	7/19/1899
Tischmacher, Joseph G.	3/19/1882	3/24/1906
Tobojek, Helen	6/9/1909	10/14/1909

Name	Birth	Death
Tomalis, Aldona M. d/o Alex & Mary Tomalis.	1928	1928
Tomaszewska, ?	3/19/1863	9/27/1914
Tomaszewska, Helena A.	2/23/1897	12/29/1911
Tomaszewski, ?	8/24/1860	1/2/1913
Tomaszewski, Czeslaw	7/6/1889	5/26/1904
Tomaszewski, Jacob	7/2/1847	3/2/1917
Tomaszewski, Mary J.	1861	1942
Tomaszewski, W.	NBDR	NDDR
Tomeo, Antonio	5/10/1913	3/9/1914
Toole, Mary M.	1899	1979
Torcivia, Santao	1882	1934
Torcivia, Sebastiana	4/18/1917	8/30/1918
Torcivia, Sabastino	8/10/1883	1/22/1912
Torpey, Anna (nee Galligher) w/o John Torpey.	NBDR	3/21/1922
Torpey, Bridget F. d/o John & Anna (nee Galligher) Torpey.	3/8/1876	7/8/1891
Torpey, John h/o Anna (nee Galligher) Torpey.	NBDR	6/13/1935
Torpey, John Joseph s/o John & Anna Torpey.	NBDR	7/13/1923
Torpey, Thomas F.	12/30/1878	6/25/1937
Toth, Juliana	2/16/1831	1897
Toth, ?	NBDR	NDDR
Tovey, Sister Mary Calista Sister of Charity, Perth, Canada.	10/16/1851	11/11/1893
Trabosh, John s/o Joseph & Rose Trabosh.	1932	1954
Trabosh, Joseph h/o Rose Trabosh.	1906	1957
Trabosh, Rose	1909	1959
Tracey, Caroline w/o Thomas Tracey.	1857	1915
Tracey, Catherine T.	1880	1969
Tracey, Joseph A.	8/23/1870	2/24/1928
Tracey, Thomas h/o Caroline Tracey.	1/15/1856	6/20/1894
Traub, Helena	5/10/1812	1/19/1873
Trieller, Catharina d/o John & Esther Trieller.	1851	Dec. 1851

Troilo, V. C. Elizabeth (nee Pepe)	1906	NDDR
Troilo, Robert E.	1907	1954
Trouffner?, Joseph	1851	7/27/1852
s/o Martin Trouffner? & Maria Wittmeyer.		
Trout, Catharine	1/6/1850	3/21/1895
Trout, Joseph I.	3/21/1858	4/5/1858
Trout, Mary	3/24/1858	4/3/1858
Trout, William D.	2/16/1851	6/1/1868
Tsitchey, Mary E.	8/8/1897	11/8/1898
d/o Eugene & Anna Tsitchey.		
Tuec, Frank	1871	2/26/1903
Tuec, John	7/18/1903	8/18/1903
Tulley, Bridget	1849	1924
Tulley, Matthew	1840	1913
Tulley, Matthew J.	1877	1940
Tulley, Patrick J.	1/23/1868	7/7/1870
Tulley, Rose M.	1875	1965
Turrisi, Rosa	1893	1942
Twardowski, Bronislawa	1847	1911
w/o Martin Twardowski.		
Twardowski, Martin	1829	1896
h/o Bronislawa Twardowski.		

- U -

Umbrella, Maria Grazia	2/21/1879	8/20/1917
Undheim, Louisa (nee Impink)	10/30/1854	8/10/1889
d/o John & Katie Impink.		
Urban, Clement J.	1856	1910
Urban, Katharine L.	1857	1924
Urso, Frank	1908	1912
Urso, Mary	1899	1924

- V -

Vazakas, Margaret M.	1870	1940
Vispico, Vincenzp	3/23/1880	3/23/1918
Vochatzer, Eleanora	1854	1936
d/o Rudolph & Philippena Vochatzer.		
Vochatzer, Philippena	1811	1894
w/o Rudolph Vochatzer.		

Vochatzer, Rudolph	1819	1909
h/o Philippena Vochatzer.		
Vondrach, Ludovica,	1852	Sept. 1853
d/o John Vondraach & Ludovica Shwenk.		
Vogel, Aloysius	1/22/1860	11/11/1868
Vogel, Daniel S.	7/15/1848	11/10/1863
s/o Felix & Margaret Vogel.		
Vogel, Elizabeth	2/25/1869	6/1/1910
d/o Nicholas Vogel.		
Vogel, Elizabeth	5/8/1850	1/21/198?
w/o Nicholas Vogel.		
Vogel, Felix	1/13/1816	3/25/1866
h/o Margaret Vogel.		
Vogel, Joseph N.	11/22/1876	4/28/1917
s/o Nicholas & Elizabeth Vogel.		
Vogel, Lucy	6/15/1844	10/26/1895
Vogel, Lucy E.	4/14/1851	4/3/1873
d/o Felix & Margaret Vogel.		
Vogel, Margaret	10/6/1821	7/25/1894
w/o Felix Vogel.		
Vogel, Nicholas	12/5/1843	6/26/1895
h/o Elizabeth Vogel.		
Vogel, William	5/4/1842	1/31/1902
Vogelmann, Joseph	1846	1897
h/o Lena Vogelmann.		
Vogelmann, Lena	1856	1920
w/o Joseph Vogelmann.		

- W -

Wachowiak, Katarzyna	9/2/1853	5/1/1927
Washowiak, Walenty	1/3/1853	3/6/1912
Wagenblast, Ellen M.	1866	1938
Wagenblast, Jeannette	9/12/1838	10/20/1876
Wagenblast, John F.	1866	1907
Wagner, Abby	4/7/1851	5/8/1861
d/o Martin & Catharine Wagner.		
Wagner, Barbara	3/21/1825	2/27/1908
w/o Georg Wagner.		
Wagner, Georg	6/21/1823	10/26/1876
h/o Barbara Wagner.		
Wagner, Heinrich	7/21/1858	2/1/1876
s/o Georg & Barbara Wagner.		
Wagner, Margarite	3/30/1899	6/5/1904
Wagner, Martin L.	6/18/1815	1/25/1867
Born, Unselsing, Konigreich, Bavaria, Germany.		
h/o Catharina Wagner.		

Wagner, Mary	1849	1899
Wagner, Paul	9/1/1901	4/26/1910
Wagner, William	1840	1890
Walatkawi, Helen	7/22/1881	10/24/1914
Wallmeyer, Gerhardus	Nov. 1811	6/11/1861
Walsh, Catharine A.	8/8/1867	4/3/1904
d/o Michael & Ellen Walsh.		
Walsh, Ellen	1/6/1832	9/3/1904
w/o Michael Walsh.		
Walsh, Michael	9/12/1816	7/7/1888
h/o Ellen Walsh.		
Walsh, Susan M. (nee Barrasso)	1913	1954
Walsh, Thomas	9/30/1858	10/24/1892
s/o Michael & ellen Walsh.		
Walter, Caspar	11/14/1829	3/27/1907
Walter, Mary E.	NBDR	NDDR
Orphan.		
Walter, Willie	10/25/1858	7/21/1859
s/o William & Mary Walter.		
Walters, Anna	1866	1944
Walters, Casper	1857	1930
Walters, John F.	5/4/1820	10/13/1904
Member of Co I 179th Pa Inf Regt Mexican War.		
Walters, Sarah Ann	12/25/1835	NDDR
Ward, Mother Mary Jerome	NBDR	5/20/1869
Warfel, Mary E.	1876	3/23/1898
Warkoczewski, Alexander	1867	1912
Warkoczewski, Anthony	1844	1916
Warkoczewski, Vitorya	1841	1917
Warkoczewski, Antoni	1874	1954
Warkoczewski, Helena	1886	1975
Warner, Albert R.	1929	1947
Warner, Margarett M.	1908	6/9/1932
Wean, Eliza	10/11/1837	12/6/1900
Wean, Joseph	11/11/1832	11/16/1906
Wean, Saloma	10/23/1874	1877
Wehninger, Albert C.	1872	1940
Wehninger, Annie T.	1870	1955
Weiherer, Andrew	NBDR	NDDR
h/o Kate Weiherer.		

Weiherer, Kate w/o Andrew Weiherer.	6/29/182?	8/26/188?
Weis, Alice L. (nee Ganter) w/o George E. Weis.	1877	1902
Weis, Andrew Born, Simonswald, Baden, Germany. h/o Pauline Weis.	9/7/1829	5/2/1882
Weis, Augustus h./o Caroline Weis.	12/8/1839	7/28/1898
Weis, Caroline w/o Augustus Weis.	NBDR	NDDR
Weis, Edward	4/20/1838	3/5/1904
Weis, Karl s/o Andrew & Pauline Weis.	1/6/1869	1/23/1871
Weis, Pauline w/o Andrew Weis.	1/20/1835	9/12/1918
Weiser, Elizabeth (nee Cassidy)	8/23/1883	4/20/1933
Whalen, Catharine w/o Nicholas Whalen.	NBDR	5/5/1919
Whalen, Nicholas h/o Catharine Whalen.	NBDR	5/13/1907
Whitman. Rose Veronica	3/2/1886	5/14/1946
Wichlacz, Anthony	1851	1937
Wichlacz, Mary	1856	1957
Wiedemier, Anna aged 6 months d/o Heinrich & Mary Wiedemier.	NBDR	NDDR
Wiedemier, Diana aged 7 years	NBDR	NDDR
Wiedemier, Heinrich h/.o Mary Wiedemier.	4/29/1831	NDDR
Wiedemier, Lucetta aged 4 years	NBDR	NDDR
Wiedemier, Mary aged 9 years	NBDR	NDDR
Wiedemier, Mary w/o Heinrich Wiedemier.	1834	5/11/1871
Wielandt, ?	NBDR	9/18//1882
Wielandt, ?	1883	1900
Wielandt, Fred P.	1888	1921
Wielandt, Frederick	1851	1923
Wielandt, Hannah	1855	1906
Wielandt, Nicholas W.	12/31/1878	12/13/1884
Wielandt, William G.	1885	1908
Willi, Anna Maria w/o John Willi.	12/16/1824	6/28/1897
Willi, Engelbert s/o John & Anna Maria Willi.	11/16/1850	8/20/1882
Willi, Godfred	1856	1871

Willi, Henry	7/6/1866	4/8/1885
s/o John & Anna Maria Willi.		
Williams, Ann	5/2/1834	3/7/1913
w/o George Williams.		
Williams, Annie	1854	1947
Williams, George	2/22/1834	8/10/1913
h/o Ann Williams.		
Williams, George	1863	1931
Williams, John	10/14/1868	10/24/1874
Williams, Joseph	3/27/1873	10/24/1874
Williams, Jospehine	12/8/1859	5/20/1879
Wilson, Agnes May (nee Mullet)	1881	1906
Wingert, Anna C.	1/21/1821	8/25/1900
Wingert, Henry C.	9/20/1838	10/14/1873
Winter, Eliza	NBDR	7/17/1886
w/o Joseph Winter.		
Winter, George	NBDR	12/12/1886
s/o George & Eliza Winter.		
Winter, Joseph	1787	10/21/1869
h/o Eliza Winter.		
Winterhalter, Rose M.	1898	1948
Wisniewski, Edward aged 1-4-0	NBDR	NDDR
Wisniewski, Franciszth	1864	1898
Wisniewski, Lucia	1906	1932
Wisniewski, Mary Ann aged 11 months.	NBDR	NDDR
Witman, John	1828	8/16/1913
h/o Mary (nee Kern) Witman.		
Witman, Mary (nee Kern)	1828	3/11/1911
w/o John Witman.		
Wixon, Margaret M.	1907	NDDR
Wixon, Raymond S.	1906	1970
Wojszwillo, Walentz	1880	1921
Wolf, Barbara	1/12/1834	1/11/1877
Wolf, Bernard Lee	2/28/1915	12/14/1915
Wolf, Catharine H.	9/13/1861	4/3/1905
Wolf, Eugene G.	1916	1933
Wolf, Francis X.	1/26/1857	7/12/1924
Wolf, Henry	11/28/1870	4/6/1906
Wolf, John	1825	1899
Wolf, Mary A.	8/5/1830	3/20/1830
Wolf, Mary E.	1883	1970
Wolf, Na ?	6/18/1830	8/8/1913
Wolf, Paul O.J.	2/7/1913	10/1/1913

Name	Birth	Death
Wolf, William A.	1882	1915
Wolf, William J.	1/8/1868	8/7/1903
Wolfersberger, Ralph L	1898	1973
Wolfersberger, Rox M. (nee Amoroso)	1913	NDDR
Wolicka, Karolina	9/12/1904	7/11/1905
Wolicki, Aleksandra	1885	1932
Wolicki, Michael	1882	1962
Wolicki, Michael E.	1909	1910
Wolicki, Rysrard M.	1917	1919
Wolicki, Tadeusz K.	1912	1913
Wolniewicz, Antoni	1853	1907
Wolniewicz, Franciszka	1861	1929
Wolter, Hildegard	5/30/1827	8/2/1890
Wolter, William	2/15/1830	7/24/1896
Woyton, Mary R.	1880	1942
Woyton, Paul	1872	1937
Woyton, Theodore V.	1909	1948
Wrede, Anna M.	NBDR	NDDR
d/o Christian & Barbara (nee Henrich) Wrede.		
Wrede, Barbara (nee Henrich)	8/15/1869	3/19/1942
w/o Christian Wrede.		
Wrede, Christian A.	NBDR	NDDR
s/o Christian & Barbara (nee Henrich) Wsrede.		
Wrede, Christian	8/17/1866	10/7/1938
h/o Barbara (nee Henrich) Wrede.		
Wrede, Marie A. (nee Shipper)	1895	1918
Wrede, Marie M.	NBDR	NDDR
d/o Christian & Barbara (nee Henrich) Wrede.		
Wrede, Paul J.	NBDR	NDDR
s/o Christian & Barbara (nee Henrich) Wrede.		
Wrede, Raymond J.	NBDR	NDDR
s/o Christian & Barbara (nee Henrich) Wrede.		
Wummer, Agnes K.	12/9/1886	3/27/1905
Wummer, Charles Peter	7/?/1827	7/23/1870
Wummer, Elias	5/2/1850	1/9/1923
Wummer, George F.	9/10/1825	3/17/1879
Wummer, Rebecca	11/3/1853	10/2/1924
Wunderly, Michael	9/29/1835	3/3/1898
Wunderly, Margaretha (nee Oswald)	1867	1936
Wunderly, Joseph H.	2/19/1866	5/1/1934

-Y-

Name	Birth	Death
Yeager, Andrew	11/29/1850	6/12/1895
h/o Elizabeth Yeager.		
Yeager, Elizabeth	10/27/1851	2/15/1926
w/o Andrew Yeager.		
Yetzer, Catharine	1821	6/29/1903
w/o Joseph Yetzer.		
Yetzer, Emma	1862	1943
Yetzer, Joseph	1827	2/16/1887
h/o Catharine Yetzer.		
Yoshida, Marie Ann (nee Conrad)	1912	1980
Yoshida, Y. Vincent M.D.	1900	1974
Young, Catharine	6/13/1827	7/26/1906
w/o John Young.		
Young, John	12/25/1819	7/21/1892
h/o Catharine Young.		

-Z-

Name	Birth	Death
Zajdowicz, John	1882	1942
Zajdowicz, Matilda	1893	1928
Zavidzki, Mary	1883	1904
Zawidski, Anna	1845	1920
Zawidzki, Anna M.	1889	1961
Zawidzki, Joseph	1841	1916
Zawidzki, Joseph J.	1880	1962
Zawidzki, Rose	1881	1962
Zawidzki, Theresa	1913	1921
Zborowski, B.	1/18/1851	10/7/1913
w/o W. Zborowski.		
Zborowski, W.	5/15/1845	10/21/1924
h/o B. Zborowski.		
Zdravecki, Andrew	1859	1941
Zdravecki, Andrew J.	1894	1964
Zdravecki, John Zerbe	1888	1923
First Sergeant Co A 33rd Inf Regt.		
Zdravecki, Katherine	1896	1974
Zdravecki, Maria	1862	1933
Zellner, Jacob	4/17/1828	1/26/1878
Zellner, Margretha	7/15/1841	11/8/1915
Zimmerman, Ella	1856	1878
Zimmerman, Felix	1844	1914

Name		
Zimmerman, Frederick S.	1873	1937
Zimmerman, Mary	1846	1911
Zimmerman, Mary R.	1882	1963
Zimmerman, Sarah	NBDR	NDDR
Orphan.		
Zint, Franzista	2/14/1827	5/11/1906
Zint, Friedrich	7/15/1824	2/15/1891
Zomreta, Zofiza Csech	1896	5/17/1900
Zuchowski, Michael	1867	1906
Zullo, Antonio	1843	1916
Zullo, Maria	4/20/1859	1906
Zychewicz, Theodore C.	1912	1972

These grave markers
were read and rcorded
By: Edgar H. Zimmerman
    Summer of 1990

Cross-Reference Index to St. Peter's Cemetery Records

Each surname in the general section is cross-referenced to the alphabetically listed name for easy finding. This index includes maiden names and possible family name cross references Possible variant spellings are also cross-referenced for your convenience. First names in some of the longer entries have been abbreviated to enable a one-line entry.